INDIA EXPRESS

FOR PARVATI, VIJAY AND PADMINI

INDIA EXPRESS

FRESH AND DELICIOUS RECIPES FOR EVERY DAY

RUKMINI IYER

CONTENTS

INTRODUCTION

The idea for this book came about from a conversation with my parents, talking about the train journeys they used to take when they lived in India. With her pinpoint accuracy for all things food-related, Mum described in detail the amazing things they'd eat on the train, from homemade picnics packed by my grandmother to elaborate meals served by white-coated waiters in dining cars. It sounded so good that I was inspired to take a trip with them to India to recreate one of their journeys, from Mum's hometown Kolkata (formerly Calcutta) to Dad's native Chennai (formerly Madras) on the Coromandel Express. The plan was to eat everything in sight, learn family recipes from both East and South India, and work out ways to incorporate them into a book of everyday recipes. So the 'Express' in this book's title reflects the original train journey inspiration for the book, as well as the speed and ease of the recipes I've chosen for it.

You may find that the vegetarian, vegan and fish dishes in this book are quite different in style from the Indian food you're used to eating and cooking. All Indian states have unique and distinct food cultures, and curries from Tamil Nadu and West Bengal are no exception – you can read more about the style of cooking from both regions on pages 135 and 159. But the common theme of the recipes I've chosen from both regions is that they can be pulled together easily on a weeknight after work with just a few storecupboard spices. That's the way that I ate them growing up – with Mum working full-time as a GP, yet still somehow putting an amazing variety of Indian vegetarian meals on the table. With that in mind, two go-to chapters of this book are made up of one-tin and one-pan curries – easy to pull together, with minimal washing-up. These recipes, like the one-tin spiced roasted paneer with tomatoes & peppers (page 108), chilli, coconut & lime salmon with roasted cherry tomatoes (page 100) or the South Indian puy lentil & broccoli stir fry (page 122) are loosely based on familiar flavours from home, but reinterpreted to reflect the way I cook in my kitchen.

The next chapters in the book focus on the authentic everyday food of Tamil Nadu and West Bengal, albeit keeping to the quick and easy theme. Many of these recipes come from my late Tamilian and Bengali grandmothers, handwritten on airmail paper, or recreated from memory. I've included my favourites, for example the molagu rasam on page 150, the Tamilian equivalent of chicken soup to cure a cold, albeit entirely vegan – it's a punchy black pepper and tamarind broth. The Keralan coconut & curry leaf potatoes with tiny chickpeas on page 138 are always a hit, and the Bengali chapter includes simple but ridiculously moreish dishes like baby aubergines with yogurt & nigella seeds (page 176) and lightly spiced Bengali cabbage & potato curry (page 170).

For keen cooks or those looking for more adventurous dishes, there's a chapter of weekend projects, where you'll find tips on safe deep-frying alongside some of my all-time favourite Indian classics – like puris and crispy fried aubergine (pages 192 and 193) or methu vada, which are fluffy fried lentil doughnuts (page 204), along with rich festival dishes like saffron, almond & paneer pulao (page 210). There's a how-to section on homemade paneer (just two ingredients, and so easy to do!), and the book finishes with a mixture of authentic desserts, like sweet pongal – South Indian rice pudding with jaggery & cashew nuts (page 226), along with some of my own creations, like the saffron & cardamom bread & butter pudding on page 230, mango, stem ginger & lime ice cream on page 232 or the cardamom, yogurt & pistachio ice cream on page 234.

The recipes in the book are largely vegetarian and vegan, as that's the home-cooked Indian food that I grew up with and am most comfortable cooking. But you'd be hard-pressed to write a book of authentic Bengali recipes without including fish – a state-wide obsession – so you'll find some of my favourite prawn and fish dishes here too. I hope these recipes, from lazy brunches to easy weeknight curries and weekend feasts, will become a part of your go-to everyday repertoire, as they have in my house.

INDIA

WEST
BENGAL

KOLKATA

CHENNAI

TAMIL
NADU

KERALA

MY FAMILY, FOOD & TRAIN TRAVEL

As a schoolboy, my father travelled the 1,000 miles from his hometown in Tamil Nadu to West Bengal on the sleeper train: he would later meet my mother there, at medical school in Kolkata. If you've met anyone from Bengal, you'll know that cooking, eating, planning what to eat next, eating what you've planned and then talking about the next meal are local pastimes. South Indians take their food pretty seriously too – Dad would be well equipped for the 36-hour train journey with snacks sent by my grandmother. An excellent cook, she'd make and pack golden homemade banana chips, crisp and so wafer-thin that you could almost see through them, vadas (crispy lentil doughnuts) and murukku (crunchy rice and lentil twists) – all deep-fried, and all completely delicious – you can find her recipes for them on pages 204 and 202. For the next course, there might be idlis (fluffy steamed rice cakes) and coconut chutney with mustard seeds, wrapped neatly in banana leaves – convenient, eco-friendly and lending wonderful flavour and scent to the food.

Railway trips from Kolkata, where my mother's family lived, would vary from home-cooked food to more elaborate bought train picnics. In true Bengali style, lunch could be a cultural mash-up of anything from tiffin boxes filled with luchis (like puris, but made with white flour; page 192) with a cauliflower & potato curry, fragrant with fenugreek and nigella seeds (page 166) to food delivered to the train from a favoured hotel – boiled eggs with twists of salt, bread and butter, fresh fruit and slices of cake. On a journey my mother took from Kolkata to a town near Punjab in the late 1950s, white-uniformed waiters would serve two to three-course meals to your seat, either Bengali or continental food – rich mutton curry, rice and dal for the former, or chicken soup, crumbed and fried fish, chips and a pot of ketchup for the latter. Mum still remembers – more than 60 years on – that the chips were thick-cut, and the soup rather thin.

My father's face still lights up when he talks about the first train journey he took with my mother, because by then, a new service had started – the Coromandel Express, a brand-new train taking just 24 hours between Kolkata and Chennai, rather than the previous 36-hour train. It was also a rather unusual trip, given that it was unconventional for a couple in India to travel together unmarried in the 1970s. Presciently, he'd told her about the superlative quality of my grandmother's cooking, and Mum packed her bags on the spot. Then there was the trip they took after they married, stopping in the state of Andhra Pradesh for lunch at the station restaurant. The waiter, keen to ensure that the newlyweds were well fed, stood over their table, ladling out more and more food, urging them to eat. Too polite to refuse, they complied – but the food of Andhra is known for its tongue-burning levels of spice. My mother had the worst heartburn of her life – so with minutes to spare before the train pulled away, my father gallantly ran up and down the platform in search of antacid from the station pharmacy. To this day, they cook with only the barest pinch of chilli, as do I – so you may find the recipes in this book rather milder than you'd expect. My family visits to India since childhood have always – slightly embarrassingly – involved a pot of yogurt on the table so I could counter the levels of chilli heat.

If you were to pick recipes from this book for your own train picnic, I would suggest the following:

IN A THERMOS
Classic condensed milk or hot chocolate chai (page 20)

TO SNACK
Easy: Cheddar, cumin & nigella seed straws (page 28)
Project cooking: Murukku (page 202)

FOR LUNCH
Mini's masala frittata (page 48)
Chilli & cheese stuffed parathas (page 56)

SWEET SNACKING
Sticky spiced popcorn with dates, caramel & sea salt (page 24)
Really superb peanut brittle (page 228)

22-5-'87

Dear Kumar and Parvati,

Received your letter glad to know all the news from your side. Happy to see Rukmini's nice drawing. I am writing below the recipe for methu vadai.

1. one cup of urd dall.
2. small bit of ginger (5 grms)
3. Three green chillies
4. salt to taste
5. Oil for frying.

For a cup of dall you can have 10 vadas. Soak the dall in warm water for 4 or 5 hours. Then grind the soaked dall nicely putting little water so that you will have thick paste. Cut the ginger and chillies in small pieces, add salt (after grinding) put the curry leaves and mix all these with paste nicely. Take a polythene paper, wet it, wet your hand also so that when you are shaping the vadai on the paper. maravu won't stick to your fingers.

⑤ <u>কাঁচকলা দিয়ে ডিমের ঝাল ॥</u>

Ingredients : সিদ্ধ ডিম, কাঁচ কলা, আলু, পাঁচ ফোড়ন,
মশলা : লঙ্কা (optional) হলুদ, আদাবাটা, সরষের তেল
(যত কম তেলে রান্না করা যায় তত ভাল), ধনে পাতা ॥

কাঁচ কলা ১½ ইঞ্চি মত ছোট করে কেটে, আলু ছোট
করে (আলোয়া মেপুর মত) কেটে আলাদা করে রাখি।
ডিমে ১টা ছুরির আঁচড় (যে ভাবে পটলের গায়ে) দিয়ে রাখি
সুতরাং কম। সিদ্ধ ডিম যেন (hard boiled)
সিদ্ধ করি আলাদা করে ॥

মশলা ... দিয়ে ...... পাঁচ ......
...., ... দিয়ে এই।
...... হলে, হলুদ ও আদা আলাদা
...... করি। ...... হলে
...... ও ...... রাখি। ...... হলে দেই এই
...... ও ...... দিয়ে ...... (...... দিয়ে
...... মত) ...... রাখি। (আরও রান্না
....) এই

(ডিম ...... পরে ...... দিয়ে রান্না ......) এই

.... এবং
....
.... — সুন্দর ....
...... এই ...... করি। আলু সিদ্ধ হলে ......,
হলে নামি, ধনে পাতা দিয়ে ...... ॥

SNACKS

ALL THE CHAI:
CLASSIC | SPICED CARAMEL | HOT CHOCOLATE (V)

PANKAJ'S ADDICTIVE
CHILLI PEANUTS WITH LIME (VG)

STICKY SPICED POPCORN
WITH DATES, CARAMEL & SEA SALT (V)

CAULIFLOWER, ONION & BREAD PAKORAS (VG)

CHEDDAR, CUMIN & NIGELLA SEED STRAWS (V)

BENGALI POPCORN SHRIMP (P)

CRUNCHY STREET-FOOD CHAAT
WITH TAMARIND & CORIANDER CHUTNEY (V)

SNACKS

When we took the Coromandel Express overnight train from Kolkata to Chennai, the most exciting thing – other than the novelty of a sleeper carriage – was the number of snack vendors who passed each carriage. As soon as the train sets off, the vendors start walking up and down the corridors, calling out 'Hot chai! Hot tomato soup! Aloo chop! Samosas!' Reflecting the train's departure and arrival states, they also offer vadas – South Indian fried lentil dumplings, and mishti doi – a Bengali sweetened yogurt, which comes in very pleasing little earthenware pots. Reflecting the national love of sweets and the inevitable effect of their overconsumption, I was impressed that they also served 'Hot hot chai – sugar-free!'. All of this was offered against the background of the countryside in Bengal – more green than you can imagine, with more palm trees than I've seen in my life. We passed rice paddy fields and fields growing just acres and acres of flowers, a patchwork of orange and purple and yellow. I got very excited at one point thinking I'd spotted a tiger in a field, but alas – it turned out to be a man in an orange stripy shirt.

I list the snacks the vendors were offering as if I was allowed to try any – my parents, armed for the trip with hand sanitiser and Dettol wipes, had taken one look at the catering compartment and I was banned from eating anything from it. But, as I mention in the introduction, packing train snacks is also very traditional, and our friends in Kolkata had packed us freshly made aloo parathas and little pots of yogurt for lunch, supplemented by our standard travel box of M&S cheese straws. But we'd finished all our own food by dinnertime and, like the guinea pig in *Alice in Wonderland*, I had to be sat on when the evening vendor came around offering 'Hot hot boiled eggs' and tomato soup. My reasoning was that they'd been boiled, so couldn't be that bad; the person who had Dettol-wiped the entire compartment before we were allowed to sit down (Mum) begged to differ. But after much negotiation she did let me try the chai, which was hot, sweet and absolutely perfect for a long train journey.

ALL THE CHAI:
CLASSIC | SPICED CARAMEL | HOT CHOCOLATE

Serves: 4   Prep: 10 minutes   Cook: 20 minutes

For these three at-home versions – on the basis you never know quite what type of chai you might be in the mood for – you use the same chai spice mix, and then stir in your choice of condensed milk, caramel or dark chocolate. The generous amounts of black pepper and ginger give this a real kick.

MAIN
2 inches ginger, grated
1 litre milk (ideally whole,
     but semi-skimmed works)
5 heaped teaspoons breakfast
     tea leaves

STORECUPBOARD
1 heaped teaspoon black peppercorns
½ cinnamon scroll
6 cloves
10 cardamom pods, bashed
¼ nutmeg, grated

FOR THE CLASSIC CHAI
2–3 tablespoons condensed milk

FOR THE SPICED CARAMEL CHAI
2–3 tablespoons tinned caramel
     /dulce de leche
Pinch sea salt flakes

FOR THE HOT CHOCOLATE CHAI
2–3 tablespoons condensed milk
150g dark chocolate (70% cocoa solids),
     finely chopped
Pinch sea salt flakes

Tip the peppercorns, cinnamon and cloves into a pestle and mortar and roughly grind. Add to a saucepan with the bashed cardamom pods, grated ginger, nutmeg, milk and tea leaves.

Bring the milk to the boil (watch it so it doesn't boil over), then reduce the heat and simmer for 15 minutes, stirring occasionally so the milk doesn't stick to the bottom of the pan.

Add your chosen chai flavourings (see above) and whisk them into the chai, stirring over a low heat for a further 3–4 minutes (make sure the chocolate has completely melted for the hot chocolate chai) and then taste, adding more condensed milk or caramel as you wish.

Strain the mixture from the pan into a teapot or jug, pour into your favourite teacup or mug and serve immediately.

LEFTOVERS: Store leftover condensed milk or caramel in a clean jar in the fridge. Use leftover condensed milk in coffee, as they do in Vietnam, drizzle it over hot porridge, or make roti canai (Norman Musa and Ruby Tandoh have excellent recipes). Leftover caramel is similarly wonderful in porridge or swirled through chocolate brownies.

PANKAJ'S ADDICTIVE
CHILLI PEANUTS WITH LIME

Serves: 4 Prep: 10 minutes

This recipe takes a packet of salted peanuts to the next level, and comes from my friend Mo's dad Pankaj. He's a wonderful host, so it's unsurprising that these are a brilliant pre-dinner snack to have with drinks – I'll inevitably make up a batch just before guests arrive to go with a glass of champagne (if I get to the guests first) or a chilled craft beer (if Tim gets there first). We'll also down a bowlful between the two of us on a night in with a glass of wine. You could use this seasoning on sev (chickpea noodles) too, or a packet of Bombay mix.

MAIN
200g salted peanuts
½ red onion, very finely chopped
1 red chilli, finely chopped
Big handful fresh coriander, finely chopped
Juice of 2 limes

Tip the peanuts, onion, chilli and coriander into a bowl and mix with the juice of one of the limes.

Taste, and add the juice of the second lime as needed – I like mine very limey; you may prefer a little less. You could chop in another chilli if you like too. Serve immediately.

If you want to prep ahead, keep the peanuts, the onion mixed with chilli and the juice of 1 lime and the coriander in 3 separate covered bowls, then mix everything together with the juice of the remaining lime just before you're ready to serve. The onions will turn a vibrant pink while they sit in the lime juice, which is quite pleasing. You can also add finely diced cherry tomatoes just before serving if you wish.

STICKY SPICED POPCORN
WITH DATES, CARAMEL & SEA SALT

Serves: 2–4   Prep: 10 minutes   Cook: 10 minutes

This popcorn is inspired by my friend Danielle's version of Saliha Mahmood Ahmed's recipe – an addictive mix of spiced, salty popcorn studded with sticky medjool dates and caramel. Tim and I have been known to eat a trayful instead of dinner – but if you're up for sharing it's fantastic to make for friends too.

MAIN
25g butter
75g popping corn
75g caster sugar
30ml water
150g medjool dates, stoned
   and finely chopped

STORECUPBOARD
1 teaspoon chaat masala
½ teaspoon mild chilli powder
1 teaspoon sea salt flakes,
   plus extra to finish
1 tablespoon neutral or olive oil

You will need: a saucepan
   with a tight-fitting lid

Tip the butter, chaat masala, chilli powder and sea salt flakes into a saucepan and heat gently until the butter has melted. Scrape the butter out into a large bowl (a silicon spatula is brilliant for this) and then use a piece of kitchen paper to wipe the pan out thoroughly.

Add the oil and popping corn to the same pan and cover tightly with the lid. Place over a medium heat until you start to hear the popcorn 'pop', then lower the heat and let it continue to pop for a further 5–6 minutes until the popping becomes very infrequent/stops. (Avoid opening the lid to check before then, or you risk being hit by hot flying popcorn.)

Meanwhile, add the sugar and water to a small, very clean frying pan and place over a medium heat, stirring frequently, until the sugar has dissolved. Increase the heat and let the sugar syrup come to the boil – when it starts bubbling furiously and darkens to a light amber, turn off the heat.

Tip the hot, cooked popcorn into the bowl with the melted spiced butter and use a spoon to thoroughly coat it. Add the chopped dates – don't worry that they will have clumped together, you'll fix this shortly – and, when the caramel is ready, pour that in too and mix thoroughly. Tip the popcorn out into a large roasting tin and use a spoon to evenly distribute the dates around the popcorn. Scatter generously with sea salt, leave it to set for 5–6 minutes and then dive in.

CAULIFLOWER, ONION & BREAD PAKORAS

Serves: 4–6 as a snack   Prep: 15 minutes   Cook: 10 minutes

You can make pretty much anything into a pakora – potatoes, aubergines, prawns – but I was intrigued when my mum told me about bread pakoras. Use something fairly robust, like sourdough, which retains a lovely texture inside the crisp shell. If entertaining, you can make up the batter and prepped veg in advance, then dip and fry like a pro (see page 187) with your first round of drinks. Serve as soon as they come out of the pan, with coriander chutney (page 36) or yogurt alongside. Sriracha is also a good call.

MAIN
200g gram (chickpea) flour
100g rice flour
360ml water
1 small cauliflower, cut into small florets
2 slices of good stale bread,
    crusts cut off, cut into cubes
1 onion, fairly thinly sliced

STORECUPBOARD
1 heaped teaspoon sea salt flakes,
    plus extra to serve
1½ teaspoons mild chilli powder
Pinch asafoetida (optional)

You will need: a large, slotted metal spoon
1 litre sunflower oil, for deep-frying

Tip the flours, salt, chilli powder and asafoetida into a large bowl and stir to combine. Pop the bowl on a damp tea towel (so the bowl stays put) then gradually whisk in the water until you have a smooth batter, about the texture of double cream. Set aside.

Bring a pan of water to the boil and blanch the cauliflower florets for 1 minute before draining well and rinsing in cold water. Give them a really good shake to dry off.

When you're ready to fry, heat the oil in a large saucepan over a medium heat, filling it no more than half full. Make sure the handle is tucked in so you can't accidentally knock against it. Once the oil has reached 180°C, or a cube of bread dropped in sizzles and starts to turn golden, you're ready to fry.

Tip the cauliflower into the bowl of batter, give it a stir, then use a spoon to carefully transfer 7–8 pieces of cauliflower into the pan of hot oil (drain each piece of any excess batter against the side of the bowl as you go). Fry over a medium heat for 3–4 minutes until golden brown and crisp – you'll know it's done as the oil will stop bubbling so fiercely.

Use a large, slotted metal spoon to transfer the pakoras to a plate lined with kitchen paper. Scatter with sea salt, encourage people around you to tuck in, and continue as above to dip and fry the remaining cauliflower, then the bread, then the onion to use up the last of the batter.

CHEDDAR, CUMIN & NIGELLA SEED STRAWS

Makes: lots   Prep: 15 minutes   Cook: 15 minutes

If you keep puff pastry in the fridge or freezer, you're never more than 30 minutes away from a trayful of these excellent cheese straws. The shape is reminiscent of my favourite South Indian snack, murukku, which my grandmother could hand-twist and shape perfectly from scratch. But the flavouring reflects my all-time favourite Bengali snack, nimki – addictive little puff pastry-ish diamonds flavoured with nigella seeds. These cheese straws include nigella seeds, cheddar and cumin seeds for an even more addictive snack – try to ignore plaintive looks from any resident canines.

MAIN
1 x 400g sheet of ready-rolled puff pastry
75g grated mature cheddar
1 medium free-range egg, beaten

STORECUPBOARD
1 heaped teaspoon cumin seeds
1 heaped teaspoon nigella seeds,
  plus a few extra for scattering

Preheat the oven to 200°C fan/220°C/gas 7 and line a baking tray with baking paper.

Place the puff pastry sheet on a lightly floured surface. For the flakiest cheese straws, you want the pastry to be a little thinner than how it comes pre-rolled from the packet, so use a rolling pin to roll it out evenly so it's about 5cm larger on each side, and just under 2mm thick.

Scatter half of the pastry rectangle with the cheddar, cumin and nigella seeds, then gently fold the other half over the top and press down at the edges. Roll the pastry briefly so it's flat, then cut it into 1cm strips. Gently twist each strip several times before pressing the edges together in a bangle shape, and transfer to the lined baking tray.

Continue with the remaining pastry strips, and once they're all on the baking tray, gently brush with the beaten egg wash. Scatter with a few more nigella seeds, then transfer to the oven to cook for 15 minutes until golden brown and crisp.

Cool for a few minutes on a wire rack and serve warm. Let any leftovers cool completely before storing in an airtight container for up to 2 days.

BENGALI POPCORN SHRIMP

Serves: 6   Prep: 20 minutes, plus 1 hour marinating   Cook: 15 minutes

These lovely crispy prawns are a variation on my grandmother's recipe for prawn cutlets, but skipping the most labour intensive stage. When my mum and I ordered prawn cutlets on a trip to Kolkata, what arrived were so massive I thought they were breaded, butterflied lobsters. 'Oh – that's just the size of a prawn here', I was told. 'English prawns are like little shrimp!' So I've cut out the butterflying stage, on the basis that prawns here are the perfect size to crumb and fry as they are. Fantastic with the coriander chutney on page 36, or ketchup.

FOR THE PRAWNS
330g raw king prawns
30ml (2 tablespoons) Worcestershire sauce
½–1 teaspoon mild chilli powder

1 litre sunflower or neutral oil, for deep-frying

FOR THE CRUMB
50g plain flour, plus 1 teaspoon crumbled
  sea salt flakes
75g panko breadcrumbs, crushed
1 medium egg, beaten

Tip the prawns into a bowl, and mix well with the Worcestershire sauce and chilli powder. Cover and refrigerate for at least 1 hour, or longer if you like.

When you're ready to prep, tip the flour and panko breadcrumbs into 2 separate, shallow bowls alongside a bowl with the beaten egg. (I suggest that you lightly crush the panko a bit further, as it'll help coat the prawns evenly.)

Shake the marinade off a few prawns, then dip and turn each evenly into the flour, then the egg, then the breadcrumbs – this is easiest if you use one hand for the egg, and the other for the flour and panko, or you'll end up with perfectly breadcrumbed fingertips. Transfer the breaded prawns to a couple of trays lined with kitchen paper and continue. At this stage, you can go ahead and fry, or place the trays back into the fridge until you're ready to cook.

To fry the prawns (you can find further tips on safe deep-frying on page 187), pour the oil in a large saucepan no more than half full and heat until it reaches 180°C, or until a cube of bread sizzles and turns a pale golden brown within 30 seconds. Turn down the heat to medium, then gently lower in as many prawns as will fit in your pan, leaving plenty of space around them. If in doubt, fry just a few at a time until you're confident.

Fry the prawns in batches for 2–3 minutes until golden brown and crisp. Use a slotted metal spoon to transfer them to a plate lined with kitchen paper as you go, and continue until they're all fried. Scatter with sea salt and serve within minutes of them all coming out of the pan.

CHAAT

CHAAT

The best sort of Indian wedding has a chaat station. First you pick from a selection of crispy chickpea noodles, puffed rice, cubed potatoes, peanuts and other delicious bits and pieces, then you add your choice of tart, sweet tamarind sauce, a fiery coriander chutney or yogurt (what you really want is a bit of everything). Then it's all mixed together – crispy, sweet, sour and savoury heaven: you can find my recipe for this type of chaat overleaf on page 36.

Other types of chaat include pani-puris, which are very crisp, bite-sized spherical shells, made of wheat flour. You use your thumb or a spoon to make a small hole on the thinner side, fill it with a mixture of spiced potatoes and chickpeas, and then pour in a tart tamarind broth, which is ever so slightly sweetened. Then you put the whole thing in your mouth at once (this is mandatory) and the shell explodes to give you the most incredible mix of flavours and textures all at the same time. Traditionally, pani-puris are a street-food snack – a vendor with massive pans of tamarind broth and the spiced filling makes up and serves the pani-puris at lightning speed to customers standing around him in a circle; my mum remembers having competitions with her brothers and sister as to who could eat the most in one go. We make them at home with shop-bought shells, and homemade everything else.

Jhalmuri, a type of Bengali chaat made with puffed rice, is particularly lovely, and the thing that makes it so delicious is the inclusion of mustard oil; it's peppery and completely unique in flavour. While edible mustard oil is used widely in India and particularly in Bengal, it is not readily available or recommended for import into Europe or the USA. For more information and to make up your mind if it's an ingredient you'd like to use, I recommend the chef and molecular biologist Nik Sharma's informative article on mustard oil on the 'Serious Eats' website. I have a bottle of cold-pressed Hungarian mustard oil at home and use it occasionally in dressings, as I would a good extra-virgin olive oil.

CRUNCHY STREET-FOOD CHAAT
WITH TAMARIND & CORIANDER CHUTNEY

Serves: 6   Prep: 25 minutes   Cook: 10 minutes

This version of chaat owes something to the Bengali jhalmuri, with puffed rice, and bhel puri, which uses tiny crushed puris as part of the mix. I've adapted this with supermarket ingredients: you can find puffed rice in the gluten-free aisle, and readily available mini poppadoms to replace the puris. But if you're passing an Asian grocer, do head in and grab some sev to add in – it's crisp chickpea vermicelli and has a lovely flavour and texture.

FOR THE CHAAT
1 medium potato, peeled, cut into 1cm cubes
3 tablespoons vegetable or mustard oil
2½ teaspoons chaat masala
50g puffed (brown) rice
50g mini poppadoms, roughly broken
100g unsalted peanuts (ideally redskin)

FOR THE TAMARIND CHUTNEY
50g tamarind paste (I used Bart)
50ml boiling water
20g dark brown sugar

FOR THE CORIANDER CHUTNEY
50g fresh coriander, leaves and stems
10g mint leaves
1 inch ginger
1 teaspoon sea salt flakes
Juice of 1 lime
60g natural yogurt

TO SERVE
Natural yogurt
Handful pomegranate seeds

Boil the potato cubes for 6–7 minutes until just cooked through, but not mushy. Drain well, and leave to cool before dressing with 1 tablespoon of oil and ½ teaspoon of chaat masala.

For the base mix, stir the puffed rice, mini poppadoms and unsalted peanuts together in a large bowl. Mix the remaining oil and chaat masala in a small bowl, and place it alongside.

For the tamarind chutney, mix the tamarind paste, boiling water and dark brown sugar in a small saucepan. Bring to the boil, simmer for 2 minutes, then turn off the heat and leave to cool.

For the coriander chutney, blitz all the chutney ingredients together in a high-speed blender or Nutribullet until you have a thin, vibrantly green sauce. Taste and adjust the salt.

Arrange your prepared ingredients and sauces together as a 'station'. Just before serving, mix the oil and chaat masala through the mini poppadom, puffed rice and peanut mix; think of it as a salad dressing – you want everything evenly coated. Divide into bowls and top with the dressed potato, chutneys, yogurt and pomegranate seeds. Advise everyone to mix their ingredients up in their bowls, adding more of the chutneys and yogurt to taste, and eat immediately.

BRUNCH

BLACK PEPPER BANANAS
WITH PALM SUGAR & PORRIDGE (V)

SPICED POTATO CAKES
& FRIED EGGS WITH CHILLI BUTTER (V)

MINI'S MASALA FRITTATA (V)

BEETROOT, CURRY LEAF
& GINGER BRUNCH BUNS (V)

MINI-NAAN PIZZAS
WITH LIME & CORIANDER PANEER
& ROASTED TOMATOES (V)

BENGALI SALT & PEPPER POTATOES
WITH SCRAMBLED EGGS (V)

CHILLI & CHEESE STUFFED PARATHAS (V)

QUICK-COOK MASALA UTTHAPAM (V)

BRUNCH

A proper Indian breakfast is a cooked breakfast – whether you're at home or out and about. In West Bengal, you'll often get eggs with peppery spiced potatoes like the ones on page 54 or green peas kachori – soft fried flatbreads stuffed with peas (page 198). In Tamil Nadu, you might have utthapam (page 58), idlis or dosas (page 212), which are all made from fermented rice and/or lentils, or savoury pongal, a dish of sticky rice with cashews, ginger and peppercorns. I seem to entertain my friends for brunch rather than lunch on a regular basis, in which case my beetroot, curry leaf & ginger brunch buns (page 50) and masala frittata (page 48) are often on the menu as they're easy to prep in advance, along with blood orange mimosas. The buns – bright pink! – and the mini-naan pizzas (page 52) go down particularly well with visiting children.

Unusually, black pepper is used in sweet dishes in Tamil Nadu: the first recipe in this chapter is for black pepper bananas in syrup (page 42), which my dad taught me to make. We road-tested the dish with Indian bananas, which are a little more robust and can stand up to cooking in the sugar syrup, before deciding to go with everyday UK supermarket bananas (which are Cavendish bananas, sadly chosen for transportability rather than taste). But if you can get any Indian Nendran bananas from an Asian grocer, they are really just spectacular to eat raw: the texture, sweetness and flavour are something else compared to a Cavendish – almost floral tasting.

Freshly made stuffed parathas are one of my favourite brunch foods, and a universal Indian breakfast. My aunt Anu, who lives in Washington D.C., makes the most wonderful version; on visits, I've been known to sit at her kitchen table in the manner of a chick waiting to be fed as she expertly rolled out rounds of dough, stuffed them with spiced potatoes, then gently rerolled them into flattened discs before flashing them in a hot pan. Luckily closer to home, my friend Mo's mother Jyoti makes perfect aloo parathas and let me come into her kitchen to cook with her when researching this book. You can easily adapt the recipe for chilli cheese parathas on page 56 by adding a little spiced mashed potato instead of – or indeed as well as – the cheese.

BLACK PEPPER BANANAS
WITH PALM SUGAR & PORRIDGE

Serves: 2   Prep: 10 minutes   Cook: 30 minutes

This is a lovely and unusual way to serve bananas, which my dad used to make for me with golden syrup. In South India this recipe is known as chenda muriyan, and you'd use jaggery, a lovely caramel-like palm sugar, along with freshly ground black pepper and just a hint of ginger for warmth. But you can use brown sugar, or indeed golden syrup as alternatives. Use bananas which are only just turning ripe from green, as that'll give the best texture to the finished dish. I like to serve this with porridge.

FOR THE BANANAS
100g jaggery
  or soft dark brown sugar
80ml water
Pinch sea salt flakes
¼ teaspoon ground ginger
16 black peppercorns, ground
1 heaped teaspoon butter
2 large just-underripe bananas,
  cut into 1cm slices

FOR THE PORRIDGE
80g rolled oats (not the large steel-cut kind)
400ml your choice of milk, plus extra to taste

Put the jaggery or sugar, water, salt, ginger and ground pepper in a medium saucepan and bring to the boil, stirring to help melt the sugar. Once boiling, lower the heat and simmer for 5 minutes until you have a thin syrup.

Add the butter and simmer for a further minute before adding the sliced bananas and turning off the heat. Let the bananas infuse in the hot syrup for 10 minutes.

Meanwhile, you can make your porridge: tip the oats and milk into a large saucepan and bring to the boil. Simmer, stirring continuously, for 5–6 minutes to your preferred consistency, adding a splash more milk if you wish.

Serve the bananas on the porridge, with a big cup of coffee alongside. Leftover syrup can be used as a porridge topper another day.

NOTES: If you're using jaggery, the easiest kind to dissolve into a syrup comes as a powder which looks like brown sugar – the solid mug-sized cones are beautiful but difficult to use.
If you're on a low-sugar diet, use date syrup in place of the sugar.

SPICED POTATO CAKES
& FRIED EGGS WITH CHILLI BUTTER

Serves: 2   Prep: 15 minutes   Cook: 35 minutes

This is such a lovely weekend breakfast, though I've been known to make it for myself as a post-dog walk treat on a weekday too. Helpfully, almost all the action takes place in the same large frying pan, so there's not too much to wash up at the end, and any leftover potato cakes can be warmed through in the oven the next day.

MAIN
600g Maris Piper
   or other floury potatoes,
   cut into 1cm cubes
   (leave unpeeled if you wish)
1 inch ginger, grated
1 tablespoon chopped fresh mint
3 tablespoons butter
1 red chilli, thinly sliced
1 spring onion, thinly sliced
2 medium free-range eggs
Natural yogurt and fresh coriander, to serve

STORECUPBOARD
1 heaped teaspoon ground cumin
½ teaspoon ground turmeric
½ teaspoon mild chilli powder
Sea salt flakes
Neutral or olive oil, for frying

Bring a pan of water to the boil and add the cubed potatoes. Boil for 10 minutes until the potatoes are cooked through. Drain well, then return to the pan and leave to steam-dry for 5 minutes.

Add the ginger, chopped fresh mint, cumin, turmeric, chilli powder, 1 tablespoon of the butter and 1 teaspoon of sea salt flakes to the potatoes and mash well until smooth, adjusting the salt as needed. Let the potatoes cool down until you can handle them, then take a heaped tablespoon of mash and form it into a small flat cake. Repeat until you've got about 12–14 flattish cakes, no thicker than 1.5cm. Pop them on a plate lined with baking paper as you go.

Heat a tablespoon of oil in a large non-stick frying pan over a medium heat; once it's hot, add as many potato cakes as will comfortably fit. Fry for 2–3 minutes on both sides until golden and crisp. (Don't be tempted to flip them too early, or they may stick.) Transfer to a plate lined with kitchen paper and keep warm in a low oven. Continue with the remaining potato cakes, adding more oil to the pan as needed.

Let the pan cool down a little, give it a clean with some kitchen roll, then heat the remaining butter over a low heat along with the chilli and spring onion. Fry for 2–3 minutes, stirring occasionally, until the butter is foaming and just turning brown and the chilli and spring onion are crisping up at the edges. Add a pinch of sea salt, then transfer to a bowl.

Heat the same pan with a drop more oil and fry the eggs over a medium heat until cooked to your liking. Scatter with sea salt.

Divide the potato cakes between 2 plates, and top each with a fried egg. Drizzle over the chilli butter, scatter over the coriander, and serve immediately with yogurt on the side.

MINI'S MASALA FRITTATA

Serves: 4   Prep: 15 minutes   Cook: 50 minutes

A perfect brunch dish for friends, packed with lightly caramelised spiced onions, thinly sliced potatoes and fresh coriander – you could think of this as an Indian take on a Spanish omelette. Even if you're just making brunch for two or three people at the weekend, it's worth making up the full frittata, as leftovers are perfect for working lunches over the next few days.

MAIN
450g potatoes, fairly thinly sliced
 (your choice to peel or not)
3 large onions, fairly thinly sliced
2 inches ginger, finely grated
1–2 red chillies, thinly sliced
15g fresh coriander, leaves
 and stems chopped
8 medium free-range eggs, lightly beaten
Greek yogurt, sliced chillies and fresh
 coriander, to serve

STORECUPBOARD
2 tablespoons neutral or olive oil
2 teaspoons cumin seeds
1 teaspoon ground coriander
½ teaspoon ground turmeric
2 teaspoons sea salt flakes
Freshly ground black pepper

You will need: a 25cm ovenproof frying pan,
 or a 25cm roasting tin or round flan dish

Bring a large pan of water to the boil and par-boil the potatoes for 7 minutes, then drain well.

Meanwhile, heat the oil in a large, heavy-based frying pan (if this is ovenproof, all the better), add the cumin seeds and stir-fry for 30 seconds until aromatic. Tip in the onions, turn the heat down to medium to low and cook gently for 15 minutes, stirring occasionally, until softened and lightly caramelised around the edges. If they start getting dark, just turn the heat down.

After 10 minutes, add the grated ginger, ground coriander, turmeric, chillies, fresh coriander and sea salt. Stir-fry for a minute, then turn off the heat and add the sliced, cooked potatoes. Stir gently so that the potatoes are covered in the onion and spice mixture.

Preheat the oven to 150°C fan/170°C/gas 3. If your pan is ovenproof, flatten the potatoes down and pour over the beaten egg. If not, tip the potato mixture into a flan dish or roasting tin lined with baking paper, flatten down, and pour the beaten egg over that. Season with freshly ground black pepper, then transfer to the oven to bake for 25–30 minutes, or until just set – it's done when the middle is no longer wobbly or wet when you stick a knife in it.

Let the frittata cool for 15 minutes before serving, spread with the yogurt and scattered with the chillies and coriander.

BEETROOT, CURRY LEAF
& GINGER BRUNCH BUNS

Makes: 8 buns   Prep: 15 minutes, plus 2 hours rising   Cook: 25 minutes

Curry leaves, mustard seeds and ginger are a classic seasoning combination in South India, so I decided to use them as a flavouring for these vibrantly pink buns. They were born from wanting to make something carby but fairly hands-off to serve for an Indian brunch with friends – there's a little light kneading, but otherwise the rising and baking time require no intervention. Fresh curry leaves give the most incredible flavour and you can often find them at larger supermarkets, but if you're stuck, use a fistful of chopped coriander instead.

MAIN
15 fresh curry leaves
325g strong white bread flour
4g fast-action dried yeast
150g raw beetroot, peeled and grated
1 tablespoon lemon juice
1 inch ginger, grated
100ml water
Beaten egg, for brushing

STORECUPBOARD
70ml neutral or olive oil
1 tablespoon mustard seeds
1 teaspoon sugar
1 teaspoon sea salt flakes

Heat 30ml (2 tablespoons) of the oil in a small frying pan over a medium heat; when hot, add the mustard seeds and curry leaves. Let them snap, crackle and pop for 30 seconds to 1 minute until aromatic, then turn off the heat and set aside.

Mix the flour, yeast, sugar, salt, grated beetroot, lemon juice and ginger together, then add all the remaining oil and 100ml water. Pour in the infused mustard seed and curry leaf oil, then stir together. Knead the dough by hand or in a stand mixer for 10 minutes, adding a tablespoon more water if the dough is looking dry.

Let the dough rise, covered, for 1½ hours, or until doubled in size. Punch down the dough, divide into 8 and then roll each portion into a ball, twisting the dough underneath so you have a smooth top. Place on a baking tray lined with baking paper, twisted side down, and leave to rise for 20 minutes.

Meanwhile, preheat the oven to 180°C fan/200°C/gas 6. Brush the buns with the beaten egg, then transfer to the oven to bake for 25 minutes until well risen. Let them cool slightly on a wire rack before serving with plenty of salted butter.

MINI-NAAN PIZZAS
WITH LIME & CORIANDER PANEER
& ROASTED TOMATOES

Makes: 6   Prep: 10 minutes   Cook: 40 minutes

This is a really easy snacky brunch or lunch dish, and a great way to make bought mini-naans more interesting. If you don't have paneer in, you could quite easily do this with cheddar, mozzarella or a mixture of both – the roasted tomato sauce spiked with nigella seeds does the heavy lifting here, along with the winning combination of lime, chilli and coriander.

MAIN
300g cherry tomatoes on the vine, halved
125g bought paneer, grated
1 chopped red chilli (optional)
10g fresh coriander, chopped
Juice of 1 lime
6 mini-naans

STORECUPBOARD
2 tablespoons neutral or olive oil
1 teaspoon nigella seeds
2 teaspoons sea salt flakes

Preheat the oven to 180°C fan/200°C/gas 6.

Tip the halved cherry tomatoes and their vines into a small roasting tin along with 1 tablespoon of the oil, the nigella seeds and a teaspoon of the sea salt flakes. Transfer to the oven to roast for 25 minutes.

Meanwhile, mix the grated paneer with the chopped red chilli (leave this out if cooking for children), coriander, lime juice and remaining salt. Taste and adjust the seasoning as needed.

Once the tomatoes have had 25 minutes, remove the vines and use the back of a wooden spoon to squash the tomatoes into a rough sauce.

Arrange the mini-naans on a lined baking tray and spread the tomato sauce evenly over each one, leaving a small border around the edges. Top each one with the grated paneer mixture, drizzle over the remaining oil and transfer to the oven to bake for 10–15 minutes until the base is crisp and the paneer is starting to turn golden. (See opposite – it won't melt like mozzarella, but rather crisp up.) Serve immediately.

BENGALI SALT & PEPPER POTATOES
WITH SCRAMBLED EGGS

Serves: 2   Prep: 10 minutes   Cook: 20 minutes

This four-ingredient potato recipe is a Bengali classic. Known as aloo morich, it's a dish of simply fried cubed potatoes, seasoned with just salt and freshly ground black pepper – incredibly moreish, as well as easy to make. As the pepper is the key ingredient, you do want to grind peppercorns from fresh in a pestle and mortar, rather than using a pepper grinder. Serve with lightly scrambled eggs for the perfect brunch dish.

FOR THE POTATOES
500g potatoes, peeled
   and cut into 2cm cubes
1 teaspoon black peppercorns
2 tablespoons oil, butter or ghee
1 teaspoon sea salt flakes

FOR THE EGGS
20g butter
4 medium free-range eggs
Generous pinch sea salt flakes
Freshly ground black pepper
½ teaspoon chilli flakes
2 heaped teaspoons crème fraîche

Cook the potatoes in plenty of boiling water for 6 minutes until just tender when prodded with a fork (you don't want to overcook them). Drain well and leave to steam-dry for 5 minutes.

Meanwhile, grind the black peppercorns quite finely in a pestle and mortar.

Heat the oil, butter or ghee in a large non-stick frying pan; when hot, add the potatoes, half the ground peppercorns and half the salt. Toss well to coat the potatoes in the fat, then fry over a medium heat for about 10 minutes, turning the potatoes or shaking the pan occasionally, until they're a pale golden brown and crisp all over.

When the potatoes have got about 5 minutes left, heat the butter for the eggs in a medium frying pan. Break the eggs into a bowl with the salt, pepper and chilli flakes and beat very briefly with a fork just to break up the yolks. Cook the eggs over a very, very low heat for 5 minutes, using a flat-edged wooden spoon to scrape the set eggs from the bottom of the pan. Once they're just looking set, turn off the heat and stir through the crème fraîche. Taste and adjust the seasoning as needed.

Add the remaining salt and black pepper to the potatoes, taste and adjust as needed, then serve alongside the scrambled eggs.

CHILLI & CHEESE STUFFED PARATHAS

**Makes: 8 (enough for 2 people)   Prep: 20 minutes, plus 30 minutes resting
Cook: 30 minutes**

These parathas are inspired by Seema Pankhania's epic recipe for Mob Kitchen, an amazing hangover cure. My recipe is a more everyday version – fluffy, lightly cheese-flecked parathas soft enough to fold and use to scoop up curries. They're low-hassle to whip up, and perfect with the roasted cauliflower curry on page 110 or the tamarind chickpeas on page 124.

MAIN
220g plain flour
100ml boiling water
40g natural yogurt
80g grated mature cheddar
1 red chilli, chopped
Butter, for frying

STORECUPBOARD
Large pinch sea salt flakes
1 tablespoon neutral or olive oil

Mix the flour, boiling water, yogurt, salt and oil together in a large bowl and gently bring together into a dough with a wooden spoon. Once it's cool enough to handle, knead for 5 minutes, then return it to the bowl. Cover and let it rest for 30 minutes.

Mix the cheddar and chilli together and set aside.

Divide the dough into 8 portions (half, and then half again, and then half again). On a lightly floured surface, roll a portion into a circle just larger than your palm. Hold the circle of dough in your cupped hand, place about a tablespoon of the cheese and chilli mix in the middle, and then bring the sides of the dough up around the cheese and 'twist' the edges to enclose in a neat parcel. Pat the twist down gently, then place on the work surface and roll the dough out again until it's about 2mm thick and as big as a large saucer in diameter.

Heat ½ teaspoon of butter in a frying pan over a medium heat; when foaming, add your first paratha. You're going to cook it for about 1½ minutes each side until it's a lovely golden brown.

Now while the first paratha is cooking, start rolling and stuffing your next paratha – you've got 3–4 minutes to roll, stuff and fold the next one while the one in the pan is cooking. Once the first paratha is cooked, transfer to a clean tea towel and keep the tea towel folded over it to keep warm while you cook the rest, adding ½ teaspoon of butter in between each (and a little more for the second side of each if you wish). Keep them warm in the folded towel as you go, and serve hot.

NOTE: If you're cooking with a friend or partner, you can get them to man the stove while you roll and stuff – or vice versa.

QUICK-COOK MASALA UTTHAPAM

Serves: 2 Prep: 10 minutes, plus 30–45 minutes resting Cook: 15 minutes

I'm always up for a stack of breakfast pancakes, and these moreish savoury South Indian utthapam, topped with chilli, tomato, onion and coriander are no exception. Traditionally you'd make the batter with rice and lentils and ferment it overnight, but this quick version with semolina is increasingly popular in India as you can put it together without the lengthy rise. Serve with the coriander chutney on page 36 or yogurt on the side. Double the recipe if you're cooking for more than two people.

FOR THE UTTHAPAM
150g semolina
115g yogurt
180ml water
1 inch ginger, grated
1 teaspoon sea salt flakes
2–3 tablespoons neutral
   or olive oil, for frying

FOR THE TOPPING
1–2 green chillies, finely chopped
½ red onion, finely chopped
10 cherry tomatoes, quartered
Small handful fresh coriander,
   finely chopped

Whisk the semolina, yogurt, water, ginger and salt together to form a batter, about the texture of very thick double cream. Cover and let it rest for 30–45 minutes.

Meanwhile, prep and mix together your topping ingredients and set aside.

When the batter is ready, heat half a tablespoon of oil in a large non-stick frying pan. When it's nice and hot, spoon in large tablespoons of batter (think American pancake-sized – depending on the size of your tablespoon, you may be doing a tablespoon and a half. I can fit four in my pan at a time).

Scatter over a little of the topping mixture on to each pancake and then fry over a medium to high heat for 1–2 minutes until the top starts to look set. Quickly flip each over – they should be crisp and golden brown – and cook for a further minute on the other side until lightly golden brown around the edges on that side too.

Transfer the utthapam to a plate lined with kitchen paper and keep warm while you continue with the remaining pancakes. Serve hot, topping side up, with yogurt on the side.

LET'S START WITH RICE

PERFECT BASMATI RICE (VG)

SOUTH INDIAN TOASTED COCONUT RICE
WITH CASHEW NUTS (V)

MUM'S ALL-IN-ONE SPICED TOMATO RICE (VG)

TAMILIAN LEMON RICE (VG)

GREEN PEA, CAULIFLOWER & ONION PULAO (V)

SOUTH INDIAN RICE WITH YOGURT,
MUSTARD SEEDS & CURRY LEAVES (V)

MY MOTHER'S CASHEW NUT PULAO RICE (V)

ALL-IN-ONE MUSHROOM & PISTACHIO BIRYANI (V)

YOU SAY KEDGEREE, I SAY KITCHRI (P)

LET'S START WITH RICE

Rice is an enduring love in our family. Both West Bengal and Tamil Nadu are rice- rather than wheat-growing states, so while other regions are famous for roti (flatbreads), you'd inevitably find rice rather than chapattis on the table in our house. Our states' preference for rice is so well known that while my sister Padmini worked in Delhi, a surprisingly frequent response to her half-Bengali, half-Tamilian heritage was 'Aah, you must eat a lot of rice then!' She has subsequently made vague indications that she prefers roti to rice, but as we'd have to disown her from the family, she keeps it fairly quiet.

While my mum's cashew nut pulao rice (page 76) is my all-time favourite, a meal might also consist of two types of Tamilian rice (toasted coconut or lemon, pages 66 and 70). OK, three types, because you'd probably finish it off with curd-rice – a South Indian rice dish with yogurt, mustard seeds & curry leaves (page 74). Until a few years ago, I wouldn't have considered the lack of green vegetables an issue – I'd see a bowl of buttery rice as a perfectly adequate meal. Nowadays, with a more balanced diet in mind, I'd stir through some chopped broccoli, or serve simple spinach stir fry (like the one on page 118) on the side.

The rice used in this chapter is basmati, as it has such a wonderful fragrance and texture. Do buy a good brand – I was interested to read in Bee Wilson's *Swindled: From Poison Sweets to Counterfeit Coffee - The Dark History of the Food Cheats* that due to the production costs, basmati rice is one of the most adulterated food products, with companies substituting cheaper rice mixed with just a little basmati for profit. Out of a number of brands subjected to blind tests in an investigation, only Tilda came out as always supplying 100% pure basmati rice, so that's the brand Mum and I buy. (Incidentally, the tops of my beautiful collie Pepper's paws always smell just like a packet of freshly opened basmati rice, so among her many names she's known as 'basmati paw girl'. To my knowledge she hasn't ever rifled in the rice tin, so we're mystified – do write in if your dog/collie is the same!)

People often ask about rice cookers – we don't tend to use one, as my dad and I prefer our rice to cook in separate grains, and rice cookers can make rice on the stickier side.

PERFECT BASMATI RICE

My family's top-secret tip for perfect rice, every time? Cook it in the microwave. You'll get lovely, separate grains, and it's perfect to eat straight away (stirred through with a little butter if you wish) or to use as a base for any of the fried rice dishes in this chapter. Brand-wise, we always buy Tilda basmati as it has such a gorgeous, aromatic scent – usually in bags no smaller than 5kg, as the thought of having no rice in the house is panic-inducing. And it's more cost-effective: Mum buys 20kg bags at a time. If you don't have a microwave, I include a stovetop method below.

SERVING SIZE: If your family are big rice eaters (read: Indian) you'll want 300g basmati rice to serve four people. Otherwise, 200g basmati rice will most likely do you for four portions.

TO RINSE OR NOT TO RINSE: Mum is evangelical about rinsing the rice before cooking, as it gets the starch out along with any impurities. My sister never rinses her rice, and points out that we can never tell the difference. On balance, and with a really good brand as above, I tend not to because the rice comes out 'drier', which I prefer. You decide – rinsing lentils is, however, mandatory.

IN THE MICROWAVE

TO SERVE 2–4
200g basmati rice, rinsed and drained well
400ml boiling water

11 minutes in the microwave on medium
10 minutes standing time

TO SERVE 4–6
300g basmati rice, rinsed and drained well
600ml boiling water

14 minutes in the microwave on medium
10 minutes standing time

You'll need a large Pyrex bowl and a plate which will neatly cover the top of the bowl to act as a lid.

Put the rice and boiling water into the bowl, cover with the plate and cook on medium (if your microwave's max power setting is 1000, then you want 800), with timings as above. Let it stand and serve.

IN A SAUCEPAN

TO SERVE 2–4
200g basmati rice, rinsed and drained well
400ml water or stock

13 minutes from lid on to cooked
5 minutes standing time
Spread out on a plate to fluff through

TO SERVE 4–6
300g basmati rice, rinsed and drained well
600ml water or stock

15 minutes from lid on to cooked
5 minutes standing time
Spread out on a plate to fluff through

You will need a saucepan with a tight-fitting lid (if your lid doesn't fit tightly or has a hole in it, use a sheet of foil underneath the lid).

Put the rice and water or stock into the saucepan and bring to the boil, then cover the pan tightly with the lid. Turn the heat right down and let it simmer very gently as per the timings above. Do not open the lid before the appointed cooking time. At the end of the cooking time, let it stand with the lid ajar and the heat off. You can spread the hot cooked rice out on a plate to fluff through and help it steam-dry.

SOUTH INDIAN TOASTED COCONUT RICE WITH CASHEW NUTS

Serves: 6 Prep: 10 minutes Cook: 15 minutes, plus 10 minutes standing

This is my grandmother Thathi's recipe, and it's one of my absolute favourites. With just a handful of ingredients and very little hands-on time, you're left with a pot of rice with the most incredibly complex scent and flavour. I'm happy to eat a bowl of this by itself, but it also works beautifully with the chickpeas with tamarind, kale & ginger on page 124 or aubergine pachadi on page 144. If you're cooking for fewer people, I'd recommend making up this quantity and freezing half for another day.

MAIN
300g basmati rice
600ml boiling water
2 tablespoons oil, coconut oil,
   ghee or butter
50g raw cashew nuts

STORECUPBOARD
2 teaspoons whole coriander seeds
   (see Note)
2 teaspoons black split urad dal (optional)
1 dried bird's eye chilli
   (or use ½ teaspoon chilli flakes)
40g desiccated coconut
Sea salt flakes, to taste

Turn back to page 65 for instructions on how to cook your rice perfectly in the microwave or in a pan.

Meanwhile, put the coriander seeds, black split urad dal (if using) and dried chilli into a medium frying pan and toast over a medium to low heat for about 2 minutes until aromatic, stirring frequently. Add the desiccated coconut and toast for a further 2 minutes until it's a lovely golden brown. Let the spices and coconut cool down, and then grind in a spice grinder or high-speed blender or Nutribullet until fine.

Heat 1 tablespoon of your chosen oil/butter in the same frying pan and add the cashew nuts. Fry over a medium heat for 3–4 minutes, stirring frequently, until golden brown.

Gently stir the cooked rice with the ground spice and coconut mix and cashew nuts together with the remaining tablespoon of your chosen oil/butter, along with a teaspoon of sea salt flakes. Stir until the rice is evenly coated – I do this with a metal spoon to avoid mashing the rice. Taste and adjust the salt as needed, and serve.

NOTE: You must make this with whole coriander seeds, not ground coriander (see page 86). But don't worry about the urad dal – you can use it if you have any in, but the recipe works beautifully without.

MUM'S ALL-IN-ONE SPICED TOMATO RICE

Serves: 4   Prep: 10 minutes   Cook: 25 minutes

This is a really lovely rice dish, packed with peppers and tomatoes and aromatic with nigella seeds. If you add cubes of boiled potato along with the rice for double carbs, it's easily a meal in itself. I like to use spring onions for ease of chopping, but by all means use an ordinary onion if that's what you have in. This is a great recipe to use up other veg odds and ends that you might have in your fridge – extra peppers, spring onions, cubed courgette or a bag of spinach stirred through at the end would all work well.

MAIN

3 spring onions, thinly sliced
3 cloves garlic, grated
2 inches ginger, grated
1 yellow pepper, roughly chopped
1 orange pepper, roughly chopped
200g basmati rice
300g cherry tomatoes on the vine, halved
400ml vegetable stock
Juice of 1 lemon

STORECUPBOARD

1½ tablespoons neutral or olive oil
2 teaspoons nigella seeds
1 teaspoon sea salt flakes

You will need: a large saucepan with
a tight-fitting lid

Heat the oil in a large saucepan over a medium heat, then add the spring onions, garlic and ginger. Stir-fry for 2–3 minutes, then add the nigella seeds and chopped peppers. Stir-fry for a further 3–4 minutes, then add the rice.

Mix the rice with the lightly fried peppers and seasonings for a minute, then add the cherry tomatoes, vegetable stock and salt. Stir, then bring to the boil. Cover the pan with a tight-fitting lid and reduce the heat to low. Cook for 15 minutes with the lid on – don't be tempted to lift it – and then turn off the heat. Let it sit for 5 minutes with the lid still on, before fluffing through the rice. Squeeze over the lemon juice, taste and adjust the salt as needed, then serve hot.

TAMILIAN LEMON RICE

Serves: 6   Prep: 10 minutes   Cook: 20 minutes

This is such an easy dish, which you can make with freshly cooked or yesterday's cold, cooked rice. The lemon zest and cashew nuts are my and my mum's non-canonical additions, because more lemon and fried cashew nuts make everything better. You can also make this recipe with very quickly cooked shop-bought vermicelli instead of rice, as the lemon, mustard seed and curry leaf base is a traditional seasoning for a popular South Indian vermicelli dish, known as upma.

MAIN
300g basmati rice
570–600ml boiling water
Zest and juice of 2 lemons
5–6 fresh curry leaves
Large handful cashew nuts,
    halved

STORECUPBOARD
3 tablespoons neutral or olive oil
Sea salt flakes, to taste
¼ teaspoon ground turmeric
¼ teaspoon mustard seeds
2 dried red bird's eye chillies
Pinch asafoetida

Cook the basmati rice in the microwave or in a saucepan using either of the methods a few pages back on page 65, or alternatively thoroughly heat your cold, cooked rice in the microwave until piping hot throughout. Let the rice steam-dry and cool down for 5 minutes (you can spread it out on a plate to speed this up) and then stir through 1 tablespoon of the oil and sea salt flakes to taste, then the turmeric, lemon zest and juice. Gently mix until combined.

Heat the remaining oil in a large saucepan; when hot, add the mustard seeds. As soon as they splutter, reduce the heat to low and add the dried red chillies. Stir-fry for a few seconds, then add the curry leaves and asafoetida. Give them a stir – as soon as the asafoetida darkens a little, add the cashew nuts and cook over a low heat for a few minutes until golden brown.

Add the lemony cooked rice and stir gently over a low heat until everything is combined (I use a metal spoon to avoid squashing the rice). Eat hot, or at room temperature.

SERVE WITH: This goes wonderfully with the chickpea, tamarind & kale curry on page 124, the South Indian puy lentil & tenderstem broccoli stir fry on page 122 or the avial on page 142.

GREEN PEA, CAULIFLOWER & ONION PULAO

Serves: 4   Prep: 10 minutes   Cook: 55 minutes

This is a lovely all-in-one dish – and practically a meal in itself, although you could serve it with a raita or spiced roasted paneer with tomatoes & peppers (pages 130 or 108) as part of a larger dinner if you wish. I like to use red onions for the colour – the squeeze of lemon helps keep them vibrantly pink as the dish cooks.

MAIN
2 red onions, thickly sliced
Juice of 1 lemon
1 small cauliflower, cut into small florets
Leaves from the cauliflower,
    roughly chopped
40g salted butter
2 inches ginger, grated
3 cloves garlic, grated
200g basmati rice, rinsed well
150g frozen peas
400ml vegetable stock
Large handful flaked almonds

STORECUPBOARD
1 tablespoon neutral or olive oil
1 cinnamon scroll
5 cardamom pods, lightly bashed
5 cloves
2 teaspoons sea salt flakes

Preheat the oven to 200°C fan/220°C/gas 7. Mix the red onions and half the lemon juice together, then tip into a lidded casserole dish or medium roasting tin along with the cauliflower, cauliflower leaves, butter, ginger, garlic, oil, whole spices and sea salt flakes. Mix well, then transfer to the oven to roast (lid off) for 20 minutes.

After 20 minutes, take the dish out of the oven, and whack the heat up to 210°C fan/230°C/ gas 8. Stir the rinsed rice and peas through the cauliflower mixture, then pour over the stock. Use a wooden spoon to make sure all the rice is submerged in the stock, then scatter over the flaked almonds. Cover with a lid or very tightly with a double layer of foil and return to the oven for 30 minutes. Your oven must be at the correct temperature and the dish needs to be very tightly covered for the rice to cook through in 30 minutes.

Once cooked, let the dish sit, covered, for 5 minutes before fluffing through with a fork. Squeeze over the remaining lemon juice to taste, adjust the salt as needed and serve hot.

LEFTOVERS: This keeps well in the fridge for up to 2 days, covered. Reheat thoroughly in the microwave before serving.

SOUTH INDIAN RICE WITH YOGURT, MUSTARD SEEDS & CURRY LEAVES

Serves: 3–4   Prep: 10 minutes   Cook: 20 minutes

This recipe for curd-rice is what every South Indian mother or grandmother would make for you if you were feeling under the weather – the cultural equivalent of chicken (or indeed Heinz tomato) soup. It's the perfect foil for a rich, spicy lime pickle (shop-bought is fine, though my great-aunt Leela makes a fantastic homemade one). A really soothing rice dish – I craved it at university and kept a jar of lime pickle in my room on the off-chance that there'd be rice on the menu in halls.

MAIN
200g basmati rice
400ml water
500g Greek yogurt,
   at room temperature
100ml warm milk
6–7 fresh curry leaves
1 teaspoon chopped ginger

STORECUPBOARD
1 tablespoon neutral or olive oil
½ teaspoon mustard seeds
2 dried red bird's eye chillies
Pinch asafoetida
Sea salt flakes, to taste

Shop-bought lime pickle, to serve

Cook the rice in a saucepan following the method on page 65. Let it cool down for 10 minutes, then gently stir through the yogurt and milk with a big pinch of salt. You want a nice porridgey consistency: not too dry, so add a little more milk and yogurt as you wish.

Heat the oil in a small frying or seasoning pan; when hot, add the mustard seeds. As soon as they start to splutter, turn down the heat and add the curry leaves, dried red chillies, asafoetida and chopped ginger. Fry over a low heat for a minute, then add to the yogurt and rice. Stir it through and serve warm with the lime pickle alongside.

MY MOTHER'S CASHEW NUT PULAO RICE

Serves: 4–6   Prep: 5 minutes   Cook: 30 minutes

Once you've eaten this pulao, you're going to be hard-pressed to go back to ordinary white rice. Using the microwave rice method as we do at home ensures that you get lovely, separate grains of rice and perfectly crisp buttery spiced cashew nuts. I give the traditional all-in-one method in a pan in the notes below in case you don't have a microwave, and it's still lovely, although the cashew nuts are a little less crisp from cooking along with the rice.

MAIN
300g basmati rice,
   rinsed and drained
600ml boiling water
30g butter
100g unsalted cashew nuts

STORECUPBOARD
1 bay leaf
6 cardamom pods, bashed
1 cinnamon scroll
6 cloves
1 heaped teaspoon ground ginger
1 heaped teaspoon ground cumin
Sea salt flakes, to taste

Cook the rice in the microwave using the method on page 65, or see the note below for the stovetop method.

Once the rice has cooked and finished standing, heat the butter in a large saucepan over a low heat; when it starts foaming, add the bay leaf, cardamom pods, cinnamon scroll, cloves and cashew nuts. Stir-fry gently for 5–6 minutes or so, until the cashew nuts are evenly golden brown.

Spoon the rice into the hot butter and gently stir over a low heat until it's coated in the butter. Add the ground spices and a big pinch of sea salt and stir-fry for a further 2–3 minutes. Taste and adjust the salt as needed (I like quite a bit, so I haven't given an exact quantity). Serve hot, with anything or by itself.

NOTE: If you don't have a microwave, you can do this the traditional way – take a saucepan, do the bit with the butter, whole spices and cashew nuts, then add 300g raw basmati rice and stir-fry it with the ground spices and a pinch of salt for 2–3 minutes. Add 600ml water, bring it to the boil, then lower the heat to the absolute minimum and cover with a tight-fitting lid. Let it cook for 15 minutes without taking the lid off. Spread the rice over a couple of plates to dry out for 5 minutes, then serve hot.

ALL-IN-ONE MUSHROOM & PISTACHIO BIRYANI

Serves: 6   Prep: 20 minutes, plus 1 hour marinating   Cook: 1 hour

This is a lovely special occasion dish, where the mushrooms are treated to a yogurt marinade before going through the rice. Traditionally, for a biryani you'd part-cook the rice before layering it up with other ingredients, but I've simplified this recipe so the rice cooks along with everything else. Do use the best saffron you can find – I like Belazu compared to regular supermarket brands.

MAIN
400g mushrooms, halved if large
100g natural yogurt
2 cloves garlic, grated
2 inches ginger, grated
2 heaped tablespoons butter or ghee
1 white onion, thinly sliced
50g pistachios
600ml hot vegetable stock
300g basmati rice

STORECUPBOARD
1 cinnamon scroll
5 cloves
5 cardamom pods, bashed
2 bay leaves
Good pinch saffron threads
2 teaspoons garam masala
  (page 87)
Sea salt flakes, to taste

Mix the mushrooms with the yogurt, garlic and ginger, then cover and refrigerate for 1 hour.

Preheat the oven to 180°C fan/200°C/gas 6.

Heat 1 tablespoon of the butter or ghee in a large frying pan and add the cinnamon scroll, cloves, cardamom pods and bay leaves. Stir-fry over a medium heat for 1 minute until aromatic, then add the sliced onion and cook for 7–10 minutes, stirring frequently, until golden brown. Set aside.

Tip the mushrooms into a lidded casserole dish or deep roasting tin and cover with the lid (or tightly with foil). Transfer to the oven to cook for 30 minutes. Put the pistachios on a baking tray and pop them into the oven for the final 10 minutes. Roughly chop when cool enough to handle.

Meanwhile, infuse the saffron threads in a mug with 2 tablespoons of the hot stock.

Remove the casserole dish from the oven and increase the heat to 210°C fan/230°C/gas 8. Add the rice and remaining stock to the casserole dish and stir. Scatter over the fried onion and spices, add the remaining tablespoon of butter or ghee, then pour over the saffron stock. Cover with the lid (or tightly with a double layer of foil) and return to the oven to cook for 30 minutes. Serve the rice hot, scattered with the garam masala, sea salt flakes and chopped pistachios.

YOU SAY KEDGEREE, I SAY KITCHRI

Serves: 4   Prep: 10 minutes   Cook: 30 minutes

Kitchri, the Indian staple which turned into the Anglo-Indian dish kedgeree in Kolkata, is classic monsoon-season food. As my mother explains, if you have nothing else in the house and can't go out for fresh ingredients, you'll always have rice, lentils, potatoes and an onion for this easy, one-pot dish. I like to add in smoked mackerel and a luxurious but quick chilli ginger butter with peas.

MAIN
1 tablespoon butter or ghee
1 onion, thinly sliced
2 inches ginger, grated
200g basmati rice, rinsed
100g red lentils, rinsed
350g potatoes, peeled
   and cut into 1cm cubes
800ml vegetable stock
4 medium free-range eggs
250g smoked mackerel, flaked

STORECUPBOARD
1 bay leaf
1 teaspoon cumin seeds
1 heaped teaspoon ground cumin
½ teaspoon ground turmeric
1 tablespoon neutral or olive oil
Sea salt flakes

FOR THE PEAS
60g butter or ghee
2 inches ginger, peeled and finely chopped
1 teaspoon chilli flakes
200g frozen peas, defrosted

For the kitchri, heat the tablespoon of butter or ghee in a large saucepan over a medium heat. When hot, add the bay leaf and cumin seeds, sizzle for 30 seconds, then add the sliced onion and fry over a medium to low heat for 10 minutes, stirring occasionally, until golden brown and crisping around the edges. Transfer 2 tablespoons to a small bowl and set aside.

Add the ground cumin, ground turmeric and grated ginger to the onions and stir-fry for 1 minute before adding the rice, lentils, potatoes and stock. Bring to the boil, cover tightly with a lid and cook for 20 minutes.

Meanwhile, for the peas, heat the 60g butter or ghee in a large frying pan; when hot, add the chopped ginger and chilli flakes. Sizzle over a medium heat for 2–3 minutes until the ginger starts to turn golden at the edges. Add the peas and 1 teaspoon sea salt flakes and cook for a further minute. Once the kitchri is cooked, gently stir through the buttery peas and add salt to taste.

In the pan you used for the peas, heat the oil and fry the eggs to your liking. Serve the kitchri topped with the flaked mackerel, eggs and reserved fried onion.

SPICES

SPICES

You may have a lot of the spices you need for this book in your kitchen cupboards already – to help you stock up with the spices you'd need for absolutely everything in the book, see the list below.

WHOLE SPICES

Cumin seeds
Coriander seeds
Nigella seeds
Fennel seeds
Fenugreek seeds
Black mustard seeds
Black peppercorns
Dried red bird's eye chillies
Chilli flakes
Saffron
Cardamom pods (green and black)
Cinnamon scrolls
Bay leaves
Cloves

GROUND SPICES

Ground turmeric
Ground cumin
Ground ginger (useful if you run out of fresh)
Mild chilli powder
Asafoetida

SPICES

ON GROUND CORIANDER

Coriander seeds really, really benefit from being ground quickly in a pestle and mortar or spice grinder before you use them, which is why I don't include bought ground coriander on your list of spices on the previous page. (I was told it might be exclusionary to suggest that you chuck any ready-ground coriander out of the window, but honestly, it tastes like bitter dust and I'd rather leave it out of a recipe than use it.) With freshly ground coriander seeds, you're getting beautiful citrussy, floral notes: well worth a quick two-minute bash in a pestle and mortar, or making up a batch in a spice grinder for future use.

SPICE MIXES

If you like to have pre-made spice mixes in the cupboard, here are a few that it's good to have about. Single-portion alternatives are given in any recipes needing them too.

GROUND ROASTED CUMIN

As far away from ordinary ground cumin as you could imagine – this is a wonderful spice to have to scatter over a dish at the end.

5 teaspoons cumin seeds

Tip the cumin seeds into a small frying pan and toast over a medium heat for a couple of minutes until aromatic. Let them cool down a little, then grind in a pestle and mortar or a spice grinder into a fine powder. When completely cool, store in an airtight jar for 3–4 months.

Used in salted lassi (page 220), raita (page 130), roasted cumin & lemon shortbread (page 236).

PANCH PHORON: BENGALI FIVE-SPICE

This typically Bengali spice mix is such a lovely, aromatic addition to dishes; you'll find it in some supermarkets, but it's also easy to make at home.

1 tablespoon nigella seeds
1 tablespoon mustard seeds
1 tablespoon fennel seeds
1 tablespoon black cumin seeds (or use regular cumin seeds)
1 tablespoon fenugreek seeds

Mix all the seeds together and store in an airtight jar until needed.

Used in Bengali five-spice roasted squash (page 104), chechki (page 166), dimer jhal (page 164).

GARAM MASALA

You'd use this ground spice blend to finish off a dish, rather than cooking with it as you would whole garam masala (that's where you cook with the whole cardamom, cloves and cinnamon at the beginning of a dish). Scatter half a teaspoon of this over your curry at the end of the cooking process, just before serving.

15–20 black cardamom pods
8 cloves
8cm cinnamon scroll

Tip all the ingredients into a spice grinder, coffee grinder or Nutribullet and blitz until fine. Store in an airtight jar for 3–4 months.

Used in all-in-one red kidney bean curry (page 112), ghonto (page 170).

SPICES

THATHI'S SAMBHAR POWDER

Sambhar powder, used to make the sambhar (South Indian dal) on page 146, can be bought in larger Asian supermarkets or online: this is my grandmother's recipe which we make at home.

2 teaspoons oil
2 tablespoons fenugreek seeds
70g chana dal (yellow split peas)
3g black peppercorns
44g coriander seeds
5–10g dried red bird's eye chillies
    (Warning, this will be hot!
    Reduce the amount of chilli as you wish)

Heat the oil in a small saucepan and fry the fenugreek seeds over a very low heat for about 30 seconds until aromatic, then set aside to cool on a plate.

Fry the chana dal and black peppercorns together in the same pan until the dal browns at the edges, then tip them on to a plate to cool.

Finally in the same pan, toast the coriander seeds and dried chillies together over a low heat until they turn slightly darker and become aromatic. Be careful not to burn the spices – you want the heat very low.

In turn, grind the fenugreek by itself, the yellow split peas and black peppercorns together, and the coriander seeds and dried chillies together. Stir the three powders together and cool on a large plate. When cool, store in an airtight jar.

Used in sambhar (page 146) and palghat rasam (page 148) if you don't have rasam powder.

SPICES

RASAM POWDER

This seasoning mix is used for palghat rasam (page 148) but there's no reason why you couldn't use it as a seasoning for roasted vegetables. Be warned – it's very hot!

35g tuvar (toor) dal
35g chana dal (yellow split peas)
20 dried red bird's eye chillies
½ teaspoon asafoetida
40g coriander seeds
3 tablespoons black peppercorns
2 tablespoons cumin seeds

Dry-roast the tuvar dal, chana dal and dried red chillies in a small frying pan for a few minutes over a low heat until they darken. Add the asafoetida and toast for a further 30 seconds, stirring continuously. Tip on to a plate to cool.

In the same pan, dry-roast the coriander seeds and black peppercorns for a minute until fragrant, then add the cumin seeds and stir for a further minute. Remove and allow to cool.

Grind all the ingredients together in a spice or coffee grinder to a fine powder. This will keep well in an airtight jar for 3–4 months.

THATHI'S PODI (GUNPOWDER SPICE)

In South India, podi or gunpowder spice is served with idlis or dosas (page 212). You put a teaspoon or so of the spice powder on your plate, make a little dip in the middle of it, and add a few teaspoons of oil before mixing it all together – you then dip the idlis or dosas in it, a bit like mixing za'atar with olive oil and serving it with flatbreads.

1 tablespoon oil
40g chana dal (yellow split peas)
40g white split urad dal
2.5g dried red bird's eye chillies
2 tablespoons sesame seeds
Pinch asafoetida

Heat the oil in a medium frying pan. Add the dals and spices and stir-fry for a few minutes over a low heat until the dal and spices change colour.

Spread the mixture out on a plate and allow it to cool, before coarse grinding in a coffee or spice grinder. Store in a clean, dry container – if stored in the fridge, this will keep for a year.

ONE-TIN DISHES

**ALL-IN-ONE AUBERGINE,
TOMATO & NIGELLA SEED CURRY (VG)**

**CRISP-TOPPED MARINATED SEA BASS
WITH GREEN CHILLI, LIME & CORIANDER (P)**

**CHILLI, COCONUT & LIME SALMON
WITH ROASTED CHERRY TOMATOES (P)**

**BENGALI-STYLE MUSTARD FISH
WITH CRUSHED PEAS & SPICED SWEET POTATO (P)**

**BENGALI FIVE-SPICE ROASTED SQUASH WITH
CARROTS & PUMPKIN SEEDS (V)**

TANDOORI ROASTED SWEETCORN (V)

**SPICED ROASTED PANEER
WITH TOMATOES & PEPPERS (V)**

**ROASTED CAULIFLOWER WITH MUSTARD,
CHILLI & LEMON (V)**

**ALL-IN-ONE RED KIDNEY BEAN CURRY
WITH TOMATOES & PEPPERS (VG)**

ONE-TIN DISHES

I knew a few of the dishes I'd write for this book would end up as one-tin curries (seeing food through a Roasting Tin lens is pretty much a permanent state for me now), but I hadn't imagined that once I got started quite how many there would be. While oven cooking (unless it's in a tandoor) isn't a particularly authentic way to cook Indian food, it works so well for dishes which you want evenly cooked, without having to stir them stage by stage in a pan. From my favourite aubergine, tomato & nigella seed curry (page 96) to the roasted cauliflower with mustard, chilli & lemon (page 110), putting these dishes in the oven both enhances the flavour and the ease of cooking – what's not to love?

For a quick snack or to feed a crowd, the tandoori roasted sweetcorn on page 106 is always a hit. For an all-in-one dinner, try the Bengali-style mustard fish with crushed peas & spiced sweet potato (page 102) or the chilli, coconut & lime salmon with roasted cherry tomatoes (page 100).

I have it on good authority that the Bengali five-spice roasted squash with carrots & pumpkin seeds (page 104) is so simple that a two-year-old can put it together (tested by my god-daughter Rosie, who apparently very much enjoyed the process of coating the vegetables in the spice mix with a spatula, and did a nice even job of it. The oven bit was taken over by my friend Emma, who is an adult).

'Kick back, relax, and let the oven do the work' is the theme of this chapter. For the stand-alone curries which aren't an all-in-one meal, just serve with rice (page 65) or bought naans or flatbreads and yogurt.

ALL-IN-ONE AUBERGINE, TOMATO & NIGELLA SEED CURRY

Serves: 4   Prep: 15 minutes   Cook: 45 minutes

This is my version of a spectacular Madhur Jaffrey dish that my mother makes: 'aubergine in a pickling spice'. The original calls for the aubergines to be deep-fried before making the spiced tomato sauce – my mother has long since roasted off the aubergine pieces in the oven, but in this version I go one step further, cooking down cherry tomatoes under the aubergine. I was delighted to find that this makes for an extremely low-hassle, but no less beautifully balanced dish.

MAIN
300g vine cherry tomatoes, halved
2 inches ginger, grated
3 cloves garlic, grated
6 baby aubergines, halved
    (or 2 large aubergines, thickly sliced)

STORECUPBOARD
2 teaspoons nigella or black onion seeds
1 teaspoon fennel seeds
1 teaspoon coriander seeds, lightly crushed
½ teaspoon ground turmeric
½ teaspoon mild chilli powder
2 teaspoons sea salt flakes
3 tablespoons neutral or olive oil

Preheat the oven to 180°C fan/200°C/gas 6.

Tip the cherry tomatoes, ginger, garlic, spices, salt and oil into a roasting tin or oven dish just large enough to hold the tomatoes in one layer, then add the aubergine pieces.

Mix everything really well, then arrange the aubergine pieces on top of the tomatoes. If you like, use a sharp knife to score a cross-hatch pattern into the cut side of the aubergine pieces and then gently rub in some more of the spice mixture.

Transfer the tin to the oven and roast for 40–45 minutes until the aubergine is cooked through. Serve hot.

SERVE WITH: This is perfect with buttery white rice.
LEFTOVERS: Keep leftovers in the fridge for up to 2 days – this reheats well in the microwave.

CRISP-TOPPED MARINATED SEA BASS WITH GREEN CHILLI, LIME & CORIANDER

Serves: 4   Prep: 10 minutes, plus 1–2 hours marinating   Cook: 30 minutes

This recipe is inspired by the classic Bengali fish-fry, where the fish is marinated in a lovely combination of garlic, ginger, coriander, chilli and lime before being crumbed and shallow-fried. I've altered it to an oven-baked dish here for ease, but you could by all means make the authentic version as an alternative: just follow the crumbing instructions on page 30 and fry the fish for a few minutes on each side in a little neutral oil. Serve with buttery white rice.

FOR THE MARINADE
¼ white onion
1 green chilli
2 cloves garlic
1 inch ginger, peeled
¼ cinnamon scroll
3 green or black cardamom pods,
   seeds only
3 cloves
½ teaspoon black peppercorns
1 teaspoon sea salt flakes
10g fresh coriander
Juice of 1 lime

FOR THE FISH
8 sea bass fillets
60g panko or white breadcrumbs
1 tablespoon oil or ghee
Sea salt and lime wedges, to serve

Tip all the marinade ingredients into a Nutribullet or small hand blender and blitz until you have a thick, green mixture. (If you're doing this by hand, you'll have to finely chop the onion, chilli, garlic, ginger and coriander and then pound in a large pestle and mortar with the spices, salt and lime juice.)

Lay the sea bass fillets skin side down in a roasting tin lined with baking paper (you want a tin large enough to hold all the fish in one layer). Spread the marinade over each piece of fish, and then cover and refrigerate for 1–2 hours.

About 20 minutes before you're ready to cook, preheat the oven to 160°C fan/180°C/gas 4. Scatter the breadcrumbs on a baking tray and mix with the oil or ghee and a pinch of sea salt. Transfer the breadcrumbs to the oven for 10–15 minutes and toast until golden brown.

When you're ready to cook, pat the golden breadcrumbs over the marinated fish and transfer to the oven for 15 minutes until the fish is just cooked through. Serve with a scattering of sea salt flakes and the lime wedges for squeezing.

CHILLI, COCONUT & LIME SALMON
WITH ROASTED CHERRY TOMATOES

Serves: 2   Prep: 10 minutes   Cook: 25 minutes

Once you've tried this South Indian seasoning – blitzed coconut, chilli, mint, garlic and lime – you'll be putting it on absolutely everything: white fish, chicken, paneer, roasted veg. . . Here it seasons a salmon and cherry tomato traybake, forming a crust for the salmon and a wonderful flavouring for the roasted tomatoes and onions. A nice quick one-dish dinner.

MAIN
1 fresh red chilli
Handful mint leaves, plus extra to serve
2 cloves garlic
Juice of 2 limes
1 red onion, thinly sliced
250g vine cherry tomatoes, halved
2 sustainable salmon fillets

STORECUPBOARD
4 tablespoons desiccated coconut
2 tablespoons neutral or olive oil
1 teaspoon sea salt flakes

Preheat the oven to 180°C fan/200°C/gas 6.

Tip the coconut, chilli, mint leaves, garlic, lime juice, 1 tablespoon of the oil and the sea salt into a spice grinder or high-speed blender or Nutribullet and blitz roughly until the chilli looks evenly incorporated through the coconut (you'll have a reddish, greenish rubble).

Mix the sliced onion and cherry tomatoes in a medium roasting tin along with the remaining oil. Make space for the 2 salmon fillets, place them in the tin skin side down, then pat a tablespoon of the coconut-chilli mixture evenly over each fillet. Scatter the remaining mixture over the onions and tomatoes.

Transfer to the oven to roast for 20–25 minutes until the salmon is cooked through. Scatter with mint leaves and serve hot, with rice alongside if you wish.

NOTES: You can substitute the salmon for cod, haddock or another firm-fleshed white fish – it'll take about the same time to cook. To carb it up in the same tin, start by roasting off cubed sweet potato with a little olive oil and salt in your roasting tin for 30 minutes, before continuing with the recipe as above.

BENGALI-STYLE MUSTARD FISH
WITH CRUSHED PEAS & SPICED SWEET POTATO

Serves: 4   Prep: 15 minutes   Cook: 50 minutes

I've written about Bengali mustard fish before, and it's just too lovely a recipe not to include here, albeit with my favourite breadcrumb topping and a side of spiced sweet potatoes and peas. This is a really easy, crowd-pleasing weeknight dinner.

FOR THE FISH
Handful panko breadcrumbs
4 thick sustainable cod or pollock fillets
3 teaspoons grainy Dijon mustard
1 tablespoon oil, for drizzling

FOR THE SWEET POTATOES
3 large sweet potatoes, cut into 2cm chunks
1 teaspoon ground cumin
½–1 teaspoon mild chilli powder
1 teaspoon sea salt flakes
2 tablespoons neutral or olive oil

FOR THE CRUSHED PEAS
200g frozen peas
1 tablespoon neutral or olive oil
1 teaspoon finely grated ginger
1 teaspoon ground roasted cumin seeds
2 tablespoons natural yogurt
Juice of ½ lemon
Sea salt flakes, to taste

Preheat the oven to 180° fan/200°C/gas 6. Tip the sweet potato, ground cumin, chilli powder, sea salt and oil into a large roasting tin, then transfer to the oven to roast for 25 minutes.

Toast the panko breadcrumbs in a small, dry frying pan for 2–3 minutes until golden brown. Transfer to a plate to cool.

Cook the peas in a saucepan of boiling salted water for 5 minutes. Drain well, then mash roughly with a potato masher. Heat the oil in the frying pan you used for the breadcrumbs and add the grated ginger. Stir-fry for 30 seconds, then add the crushed peas and stir-fry for 2–3 minutes. Stir through the ground roasted cumin seeds, yogurt and lemon juice, then taste and add salt as needed. Set aside.

Once the potatoes have had 25 minutes, remove them from the oven, and make space for the 4 fish fillets. Spread the mustard over each piece of fish and top with the toasted breadcrumbs. Drizzle over the oil, then transfer to the oven to bake for 20–25 minutes until the top is just golden brown and the fish is cooked through. Serve the fish and chipped sweet potatoes with the crushed peas on the side.

NOTE: See page 86 for more on ground roasted cumin seeds. It's such a versatile seasoning and takes minutes to make – a million miles from ordinary ready-ground cumin.

BENGALI FIVE-SPICE ROASTED SQUASH WITH CARROTS & PUMPKIN SEEDS

Serves: 4   Prep: 10 minutes   Cook: 50 minutes

I make so many versions of roasted squash – this one with a garlic, ginger and Bengali five-spice crust is a new favourite. You can find panch phoron (literally 'five-spice') in larger supermarkets in the spice aisle or in the Asian food aisle – it's a lovely aromatic mixture of fenugreek, black cumin, nigella, mustard and fennel seeds – easy to make up yourself in equal quantities (page 87), but I usually buy a packet of ready-mixed.

MAIN
600g squash, cut into 3cm wedges
300g carrots, peeled and halved
    (purple are nice if available)
1 red onion, cut into eighths
2 cloves garlic, grated
1 inch ginger, grated
5–6 tablespoons Greek yogurt
Juice of ½ lemon
Handful pumpkin seeds

STORECUPBOARD
2 teaspoons panch phoron (page 87),
    or ½ teaspoon each of nigella, mustard,
    fennel, black cumin and fenugreek seeds –
    or use what you have to hand
3 tablespoons neutral or olive oil
½–1 teaspoon mild chilli powder, to taste
1 heaped teaspoon sea salt flakes

Preheat the oven to 180°C fan/200°C/gas 6.

Tip the squash, carrots, red onion, garlic and ginger into a roasting tin large enough to just hold everything in one layer (a little bit of overlap is OK).

Roughly grind the panch phoron in a pestle and mortar, then add it to the roasting tin with the oil, chilli powder and salt. Mix well to coat the vegetables in the spices, then transfer to the oven to roast for 50 minutes until the vegetables are all cooked through.

Mix the yogurt and lemon juice together and drizzle the mixture over the vegetables. Scatter over the pumpkin seeds and serve hot.

LEFTOVERS: This heats up well the next day, and tastes lovely in wraps with more yogurt.

TANDOORI ROASTED SWEETCORN

Serves: 2–4   Prep: 10 minutes   Cook: 25 minutes

Why should tandoori chicken have all the fun? This is fantastic as a snack or side dish – and if you've got the weather for it, you could certainly cook it on the barbecue rather than in the oven. I like to have this as a 5 p.m. pre-dinner snack with a glass of kefir on the side.

MAIN
4 corn on the cob
2 heaped tablespoons (60g) natural yogurt
2 cloves garlic, grated
2 inches ginger, grated
2 teaspoons butter

STORECUPBOARD
1 tablespoon neutral or olive oil
1 teaspoon ground coriander
1 teaspoon ground cumin
½ teaspoon ground turmeric
1 teaspoon mild chilli powder
1 teaspoon sea salt flakes

Preheat the oven to 180°C fan/200°C/gas 6 and place the corn cobs on a tray lined with baking paper.

Mix the yogurt, garlic, ginger, oil, spices and salt together in a bowl. Slather this mixture all over the corn cobs, making sure they're evenly coated, then transfer to the oven to roast for 25 minutes.

For the tandoori effect, whack your grill up to high, dot the roasted cobs with butter and grill for 2–3 minutes on each side to get the kernels lovely and charred. Serve hot.

SPICED ROASTED PANEER
WITH TOMATOES & PEPPERS

Serves: 4 Prep: 10 minutes Cook: 30 minutes

This is such an easy one-tin dish, as good alongside rice and dal as it is with flatbreads and yogurt. You can use bought paneer as it's so easy to slice and cook and crisps up beautifully on roasting. A top tip from my fellow food writer Roopa Gulati is to soak bought paneer in boiling water for 10 minutes or so before using it – it really improves the texture.

MAIN
225g paneer
3 mixed peppers, thinly sliced
250g cherry tomatoes on the vine, halved
1 red onion, thickly sliced
1 red chilli, thinly sliced
2 inches ginger, grated
2 cloves garlic, grated
Lemon wedges, to serve

STORECUPBOARD
2 tablespoons neutral or olive oil
1 heaped teaspoon ground cumin
1 heaped teaspoon ground coriander
1 teaspoon fennel seeds
½ teaspoon ground turmeric
1 teaspoon sea salt flakes
Freshly ground black pepper

Preheat the oven to 180°C fan/200°C/gas 6.

Cut the paneer into 6 squares, and then each in half so you have 12 triangles. Halve the triangles horizontally, so you have 24 thin (rather than 12 thick) triangles. Soak in boiling water for 10 minutes while you get on with cutting up the rest of the veg. (If you've bought your paneer pre-cut, just use it as it comes.)

Drain the paneer through a sieve, and pat it dry with kitchen paper before transferring to a large roasting tin along with the peppers, tomatoes, onion, chilli, ginger and garlic. Add the oil, spices and salt and mix well. Fish the paneer pieces out so they lie on top of the peppers (this will help them crisp up), scatter with the freshly ground black pepper, then transfer to the oven to roast for 30 minutes.

Serve hot, with the lemon wedges alongside to squeeze over.

LEFTOVERS: This keeps well in the fridge for 1–2 days and you can reheat in the microwave.
MAKE IT VEGAN: You can use tofu to veganise this dish.

ROASTED CAULIFLOWER
WITH MUSTARD, CHILLI & LEMON

Serves: 4   Prep: 10 minutes   Cook: 25 minutes

In this recipe, I give my favourite vegetable – cauliflower – the Bengali mustard fish treatment. It takes just minutes to put together, and tastes spectacularly good with the parathas on page 56. If you're just serving two and fancy doing something creative with leftovers the next day, I recommend blitzing the roasted cauliflower with hot milk or stock until smooth and then heating through on the stove for a warming spiced cauliflower soup.

MAIN

1 medium cauliflower,
   cut into medium florets
1 small sweetheart cabbage,
   cut into 3cm chunks
1 red onion, thickly sliced
5 tablespoons natural yogurt
1 large red chilli, finely chopped
Juice of ½ lemon
½ red chilli, chopped
Coriander leaves, to serve

STORECUPBOARD

4 heaped tablespoons grainy Dijon mustard
2 tablespoons neutral or olive oil
1 teaspoon sea salt flakes, plus extra to taste

Preheat the oven to 200°C fan/220°C/gas 7.

Tip the cauliflower, cabbage and onion into a roasting tin large enough to hold everything in one layer. In a bowl, mix together the yogurt, mustard, oil, chilli and salt, then slather this mixture all over the vegetables until they're evenly coated.

Transfer to the oven to roast for 25 minutes until the cauliflower is just cooked through and the cabbage is starting to char around the edges. Dress with the lemon juice, scatter over the chilli and taste. Add salt as needed, and serve hot, scattered with coriander.

SERVE WITH: This is perfect with plain white rice (page 65) or parathas (page 56).

ALL-IN-ONE RED KIDNEY BEAN CURRY
WITH TOMATOES & PEPPERS

Serves: 4–6   Prep: 10 minutes   Cook: 45 minutes

This curry, known as rajma, is a classic – I ask my mother to make it every time I'm home for a birthday. In this version I bump up the veg with a whole pack of peppers, and it all goes in one tin because it's an easy way to brown off the onions, spices and veg without standing at the stove and stirring. You can, if you like, swap the red kidney beans for chickpeas for a simple chickpea curry (my sister's favourite).

MAIN

1 large onion, finely chopped
3 mixed peppers, roughly chopped
250g vine cherry tomatoes, halved
   (keep the vines)
2 inches ginger, grated
2 cloves garlic, grated
1 x 400g tin kidney beans,
   drained and rinsed
1 x 400g tin chopped tomatoes
Lemon juice and fresh coriander leaves,
   to serve

STORECUPBOARD

2 tablespoons neutral or olive oil
2 teaspoons ground cumin
1 heaped teaspoon ground coriander
1 teaspoon fennel seeds
1 teaspoon mild chilli powder
½ teaspoon ground turmeric
1 teaspoon sea salt flakes
1 teaspoon garam masala (page 87)

Preheat the oven to 180°C fan/200°C/gas 6.

Tip the onion, peppers, tomatoes, tomato vines, ginger and garlic into a large roasting tin along with the oil, all the spices and the salt. Transfer to the oven to roast for 25 minutes.

After 25 minutes add the kidney beans and tinned tomatoes, stir well and return to the oven for a further 20 minutes. Remove the vines, squeeze over the lemon juice, scatter over the garam masala and check for salt. Serve hot, scattered with the coriander leaves.

SERVE WITH: This is lovely straight away, but even better made in advance and reheated. It also freezes very well.

ONE-PAN
DISHES

PADMINI'S TOMATO, ONION & SPINACH CURRY (VG)

EASY MUSHROOM & YOGURT CURRY (V)

**SOUTH INDIAN PUY LENTIL
& TENDERSTEM BROCCOLI STIR FRY (VG)**

CHICKPEAS WITH TAMARIND, KALE & GINGER (VG)

BEETROOT, CARROT & COCONUT DAL (VG)

**SOUTH INDIAN-STYLE BLACK PEPPER
& FENNEL PRAWNS (P)**

**CUCUMBER | PINEAPPLE | BEETROOT
RAITA (V)**

ONE-PAN DISHES

This is a collection of easy stir fries that I've left as one-pan dishes rather than using the oven. Almost all of them take just minutes to prep and put together – the chickpeas with tamarind, kale & ginger (page 124) are always a hit, and I pretty much always have the ingredients for my sister's tomato, onion & spinach curry (page 118) to hand for a quick vegetable fix.

The only recipe in the chapter which takes a little longer is the beetroot, carrot & coconut dal (page 126), but it's largely hands-off time while the dal cooks. It's perfect to batch-cook and freeze or keep in portions for the week – just let it down with a little hot stock or water, as it'll thicken up in the fridge.

The chapter finishes with three of my favourite raitas (page 130) – pineapple (which I request for my birthday every year), beetroot (it's so pink!) and cucumber. By all means add some fresh mint in with any of them; I like to keep them quite plain so they don't compete with other flavours on the plate.

For a complete meal, serve any of the dishes in this chapter with rice, bought naans or flatbreads and yogurt.

PADMINI'S TOMATO, ONION & SPINACH CURRY

Serves: 4   Prep: 10 minutes   Cook: 20 minutes

My sister Padmini used to make this dish when we were flatmates – it's a lovely way to get a couple of your five-a-day in. The ground roasted cumin does the heavy lifting in this very lightly spiced dish, so it's well worth toasting some cumin seeds for this and for any other recipes that call for it (see page 86).

MAIN
1 red or white onion, thinly sliced
2½ inches ginger, grated
2 cloves garlic, grated
275g cherry tomatoes
  on the vine, halved
300g baby spinach
Juice of ½ lemon

STORECUPBOARD
2 teaspoons cumin seeds,
  roasted and ground (see below)
2 tablespoons neutral or olive oil
1 teaspoon mild chilli powder
Sea salt flakes, to taste

To make up the ground roasted cumin from scratch, pop the cumin seeds into a small frying pan and toast for 1–2 minutes over a medium to low heat until aromatic. Tip into a pestle and mortar and grind until fine.

Heat the oil in a large saucepan and add the onion. Fry over a medium heat, stirring occasionally, for 10 minutes until golden brown, then add the ginger and garlic. Cook for a further 2–3 minutes.

Reduce the heat to low, then add the ground roasted cumin and chilli powder. Stir-fry for a minute, then add the cherry tomatoes and cook for 5 minutes, stirring occasionally, until just softened.

Stir in the spinach (you can do this in two batches) and cook until just wilted. Turn off the heat, then taste and add salt as needed. Squeeze over the lemon juice and serve hot with rice.

EASY MUSHROOM & YOGURT CURRY

Serves: 4   Prep: 10 minutes   Cook: 25 minutes

This simple curry is lovely for a weeknight dinner at home with a pile of flatbreads, naan or fluffy white rice, but I'd happily serve it to friends too. If you see any interesting mushrooms in season at the supermarket or shops, by all means use those in place of the chestnut and button mushrooms suggested below.

MAIN

1 large onion, finely chopped
2 cloves garlic, grated
1 inch ginger, grated
250g chestnut mushrooms, halved
200g baby button mushrooms, whole
200g Greek yogurt, at room temperature
Handful fresh mint leaves, roughly chopped

STORECUPBOARD

3 tablespoons neutral or olive oil
1 teaspoon cumin seeds
1 teaspoon fennel seeds
1 teaspoon ground cumin
½ teaspoon ground turmeric
½ teaspoon chilli powder
1 teaspoon sea salt flakes, or to taste

Heat 2 tablespoons of the oil in a large frying pan and add the cumin and fennel seeds. Stir-fry for 30 seconds over a medium heat, then add the onion, garlic and ginger. Cook for 10 minutes over a medium to low heat, stirring occasionally, until the onions are golden brown.

Use the time while the onions are cooking to clean and chop your mushrooms.

Once the onions are brown, add the ground cumin, turmeric, chilli powder and sea salt and stir-fry for 30 seconds before adding the mushrooms and the remaining tablespoon of oil. Cook the mushrooms for 10 minutes over a medium heat, stirring frequently, until they're just cooked through.

Turn off the heat and gently stir through the Greek yogurt. Warm the curry through over a very low heat so as not to split the yogurt, then taste and add more salt as needed. Serve hot, scattered with the freshly chopped mint.

SOUTH INDIAN PUY LENTIL & TENDERSTEM BROCCOLI STIR FRY

Serves: 4   Prep: 5 minutes   Cook: 10 minutes

This is a quick and easy weeknight stir fry – if you serve it with rice or flatbreads, it's all your food groups on one plate. Tenderstem broccoli is perfect for this dish as it retains its crunch and works beautifully with the simple mustard and cumin-infused frying oil. A teaspoon of chilli flakes will give you a good kick of heat in this dish; reduce by half if you're after a milder dish.

MAIN
300g tenderstem broccoli, halved
500g vac-packed puy lentils
Juice of 1 lime
Handful salted peanuts,
   roughly chopped

STORECUPBOARD
2 tablespoons neutral or olive oil,
   plus extra to serve
1 teaspoon mustard seeds
1 teaspoon cumin seeds
1 teaspoon chilli flakes
½ teaspoon ground turmeric
1 teaspoon sea salt flakes

Tip the broccoli into a bowl of boiling water and let it blanch for 2 minutes.

Meanwhile, heat the oil in a large frying pan and add the mustard and cumin seeds. Turn the heat down to medium to low and let them splutter for 30 seconds, or until the cumin seeds start to darken very slightly. Drain the broccoli and add it to the pan.

Add the chilli flakes, turmeric and sea salt and stir-fry over a high heat for 2–3 minutes before adding the puy lentils. Stir for a further 2–3 minutes over a lower heat, then add the lime juice, taste the salt and adjust as needed and add a little more oil if you wish.

Serve hot, scattered with the peanuts, with rice or flatbreads and yogurt alongside.

CHICKPEAS WITH TAMARIND, KALE & GINGER

Serves: 4   Prep: 10 minutes   Cook: 30 minutes

This is hands-down my favourite way to cook chickpeas. The tartness of the tamarind, along with a tiny bit of brown sugar make for a really moreish dish – hot, sour and slightly sweet, perfect to scoop up with flatbreads and yogurt. If I come across a tin of miniature brown chickpeas, known as kala chana, then I often use this recipe (without the kale) to top canapé-sized potato cakes (page 194), with a half teaspoon of yogurt and a couple of coriander leaves on top.

MAIN

1 red onion, thickly sliced
2 inches ginger, grated
2 x 400g tins chickpeas, drained and rinsed
    (or 1 x 700g jar chickpeas, drained
    and rinsed)
3 tablespoons tamarind paste
300ml water
100g kale, finely chopped
    (remove and discard the tough stems first)
Roughly chopped fresh coriander, to serve

STORECUPBOARD

2 tablespoons olive or neutral oil
2 teaspoons cumin seeds
1 teaspoon chilli flakes
1 teaspoon sea salt flakes
1 heaped tablespoon dark brown sugar

Heat the oil in a large saucepan over a medium heat; when hot, add the cumin seeds. Let them sizzle for 30 seconds, then add the onion and stir-fry for 6–7 minutes until just browning at the edges. Add the ginger and chilli flakes, stir-fry for a further minute and then add the drained chickpeas, tamarind paste, water, salt and sugar.

Stir, then cover and cook for 20 minutes. After 20 minutes, add the chopped kale and simmer, uncovered, for a further 5 minutes until the kale is just cooked and the liquid has reduced. Taste for salt and add more as needed. Scatter with fresh coriander just before serving.

SERVE WITH: Delicious with flatbreads or naan and yogurt, with the chilli cheese parathas on page 56, or as a jacket potato filling with plenty of butter and grated mature cheddar.

BEETROOT, CARROT & COCONUT DAL

Serves: 4–6 generously   Prep: 15 minutes   Cook: 50 minutes

This is a brilliant 'hidden veg' dal – as an adult, I shouldn't have to hide vegetables from myself, but I get a kick out of adding extra veg to recipes to help get up to five a day (or ten a day, if that's your thing). It's also helpful if you're cooking for children. As with all Indian dishes, I like to use the time it takes for the onions to cook to cut up the other vegetables, just turning round occasionally to stir the pan, as it cuts down drastically on prep time. Coconut milk and lime juice add a richness to this easy, everyday dish.

MAIN

1 large onion, thinly sliced
3 large raw beetroot, peeled
2 large carrots, peeled
2 inches ginger, finely grated
150g red lentils, rinsed
500ml vegetable stock,
    plus extra as needed
1 x 400ml tin coconut milk
Juice of 2 limes

STORECUPBOARD

2 tablespoons olive or neutral oil
2 teaspoons cumin seeds
1 teaspoon sea salt flakes
1 teaspoon ground cumin
1 teaspoon ground coriander
1 teaspoon mild chilli powder
½ teaspoon ground turmeric

You will need: a saucepan
    with a tight-fitting lid

Heat the oil in a large saucepan over a medium heat; once hot, add the cumin seeds and fry for 15–30 seconds until aromatic. Add the onion and cook for 10 minutes over a medium to low heat, stirring occasionally, until golden brown and starting to crisp at the edges.

Meanwhile, grate 1 beetroot and 1 carrot, then slice the remaining veg into 5mm half-moons. Once the onion has had 10 minutes, add the grated vegetables and ginger along with the salt and ground spices. Stir-fry for 3–5 minutes until the vegetables have softened.

Add the lentils, stock and vegetable half-moons to the pan and bring to the boil. Once boiling, lower the heat, cover and cook for 30 minutes, stirring halfway through before re-covering.

After 30 minutes, add the coconut milk and bring the dal back to the boil, then add the lime juice and a little more stock if you prefer a thinner dal, and taste for salt, adding more as needed. (I think it can take quite a lot of salt.) Serve hot, with flatbreads or buttery white rice.

LEFTOVERS: This keeps well in the fridge for 2–3 days, and also freezes well. You may want to add more stock when reheating, as it thickens a lot on cooling.

SOUTH INDIAN-STYLE BLACK PEPPER & FENNEL PRAWNS

Serves: 2   Prep: 10 minutes   Cook: 20 minutes

This is a lovely, quick prawn curry, with a real kick of spice from the mixture of fennel, black pepper and chilli. It's no more than 20 minutes to put together from start to finish, so an easy weeknight dinner – just serve with some buttery white rice on the side.

MAIN

1 large onion, finely chopped
1 inch ginger, finely grated
7 fresh curry leaves
100g cherry tomatoes
    on the vine, roughly chopped
100ml water
180g raw king prawns
Roughly chopped fresh coriander, to serve

STORECUPBOARD

2 tablespoons neutral or olive oil
½ teaspoon fennel seeds
½ teaspoon coriander seeds
½ teaspoon cumin seeds
½ teaspoon black peppercorns
1 dried red bird's eye chilli
Sea salt flakes, to taste

Heat the oil in a large frying pan and add the onion, ginger and curry leaves. Cook over a medium to low heat with a pinch of sea salt for 10 minutes, stirring occasionally, until golden brown around the edges.

Meanwhile, tip the fennel seeds, coriander seeds, cumin seeds, black peppercorns and dried red chilli into a small frying pan and toast over a medium to low heat for 2–3 minutes until aromatic. Tip into a pestle and mortar and grind until fine.

Once the onions are golden brown, add the ground spices and stir-fry for 30 seconds. Add the chopped cherry tomatoes and cook over a medium heat for a further 2–3 minutes, before adding the water and king prawns. Increase the heat to medium to high and cook for 3 minutes, stirring frequently, until the prawns are cooked through and the sauce has thickened and reduced.

Add salt to taste, then scatter with the fresh coriander before serving hot.

CUCUMBER | PINEAPPLE | BEETROOT RAITA

Serves: 4   Prep: 10 minutes

These are three of my favourite raita recipes – they take minutes to whip up, and are perfect alongside pretty much any of the dishes in this book. You can veganise by using your preferred brand of non-dairy yogurt (I like Alpro soya yogurt for the flavour).

CUCUMBER RAITA

200g cucumber
200g natural yogurt
½ teaspoon sea salt flakes
½ teaspoon ground roasted cumin
   (page 86)
Pinch mild chilli powder

Deseed the cucumber and cut it into small dice. Stir through the yogurt, salt and most of the ground roasted cumin. Scatter with the remaining ground roasted cumin and the chilli powder and serve. Best eaten immediately – keep the cucumber separate from the yogurt if you are prepping in advance.

PINEAPPLE RAITA

160g fresh or tinned pineapple
200g natural yogurt
½ teaspoon sea salt flakes
Pinch mild chilli powder,
   plus extra to serve

Chop the pineapple into small pieces. Just before serving, stir through the yogurt, sea salt and chilli powder. Top with a little more chilli powder and serve immediately. This is best eaten just after you've mixed it – keep the pineapple separate from the yogurt if you are prepping in advance.

BEETROOT RAITA

1 medium beetroot (90g),
   peeled and grated
1 tablespoon lemon juice
200g natural yogurt
½ teaspoon ground roasted cumin
   (page 86)
½ teaspoon sea salt flakes
Pinch mild chilli powder

Stir the beetroot, lemon juice, yogurt, cumin, sea salt and chilli powder together. This keeps well if made in advance, and turns the most incredible shade of pink.

SOME TRADITIONAL SOUTH INDIAN DISHES

KERALAN POTATO CURRY
WITH CHICKPEAS & COCONUT (VG)

EASY FRIED OKRA (VG)

AVIAL
ONE-POT CARROTS, GREEN BEANS
& AUBERGINE WITH COCONUT & YOGURT (V)

AUBERGINE PACHADI (V)

SAMBHAR (V)

PALGHAT RASAM
QUICK TOMATO & TAMARIND BROTH (VG)

MOLAGU RASAM
SOUTH INDIAN BLACK PEPPER BROTH (VG)

COCONUT, TAMARIND & CURRY LEAF BROTH (V)
THAENGA ARACHU KOZHAMBU

SOME TRADITIONAL SOUTH INDIAN DISHES

My dad's parents had the traditional set-up for their generation – she did the cooking at home, while he went out to work. But in raising my dad and his two brothers, my grandmother, who we called Thathi, was cooking non-stop – a hot breakfast before school, cooked lunch sent in a tiffin box, snacks when the boys got home, and then dinner consisting of at least four or five dishes, such as the sambhar on page 146, avial on page 142 and potato curry on page 138, with rice alongside. Her only break was once every month – at that time in the South, women on their period weren't allowed in the kitchen as they were considered ritually impure. I don't know whether the roots of this lay in misogyny, or whether it was secretly started by women who just wanted a rest from cooking – I do hope it was the latter. Anyway, for a week every month, Thathi would stand at the kitchen door and direct the boys and my grandfather, Thatha, on how to prepare her recipes – not very restful, but it did leave my dad and uncles with a good working knowledge of how to cook. Dad's specialities are potato curry (page 140), coconut rice (page 66) and lemon rice (page 70) – often in the same meal. Our family has no issue with double or triple carbs.

When Thathi and Thatha lived in their house in Tambaram, in Tamil Nadu (they later moved to Washington D.C.), they were keen gardeners, growing coconut, mango, papaya and jackfruit trees and a herb garden including curry leaves. Cauliflower and cabbage feature heavily in Thathi's recipes, even though they were known as 'English vegetables' and not commonly used in South Indian cooking – she was familiar with them from the family's time in Kolkata and at a hill station in the mountainous Nilgiris, which have a cooler climate. By the time I knew them, things had equalised in the kitchen – Thatha always helped Thathi prep for dinner, and was known for meticulously chopping vegetables into exact-sized pieces. The family recipes which come from Thathi were written down by Thatha to her dictation and sometimes emailed over – he was a keen computer user well into his eighties. (When he lived with my aunt and uncle in Washington D.C., I found it very sweet that he kept a notebook of computer-related questions and answers, so he wouldn't have to ask my cousins the same question twice.)

Thathi's sister, my great-aunt Leela Chithi, still lives in India, in Trivandrum, Kerala, and we visited her on our most recent trip. She's a very spry 80, and took us trekking in the hills – I was really surprised at how similar the landscape looked to Scotland (although my parents disagreed). When we bounced down from our climb, she produced a flask of very strong South Indian coffee – South Indians are coffee rather than tea drinkers – and homemade semolina sweets, a very helpful post-exercise refresher.

Back at her house, I was allowed to help in the kitchen until my ability to make round dosas disappeared under scrutiny. I was given a chair to sit on by the stove, and instead handed a plate with her rounder, expertly made dosas fresh from the pan, stuffed with spiced potatoes and served with sambhar. You can find the recipe on page 212 – they're easy to make at home once you get the hang of it, with just a little time for the overnight fermentation, like a loaf of bread that requires a slow rise.

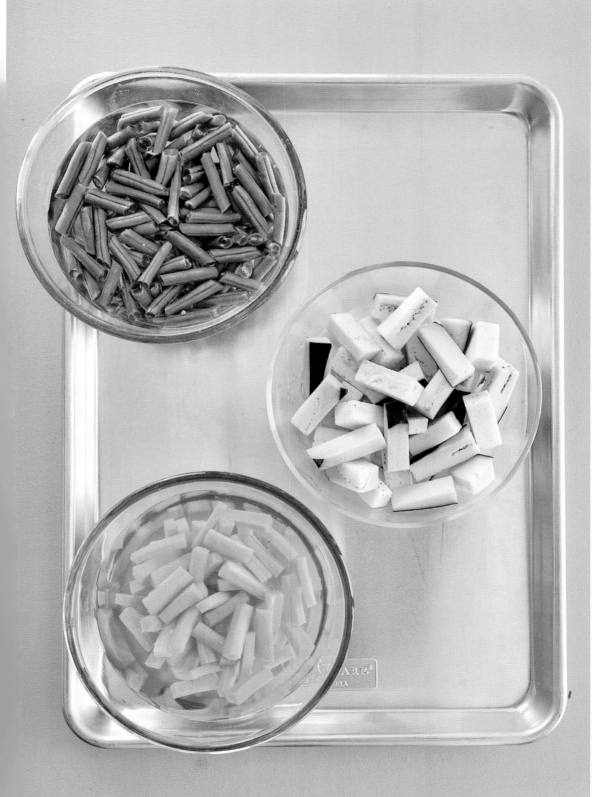

KERALAN POTATO CURRY
WITH CHICKPEAS & COCONUT

Serves: 4   Prep: 10 minutes   Cook: 15 minutes

This is a lovely quick dish, known as Ernakulam thoran. It's one of the first curries that my mum made for my dad when they were dating, clipped out from a popular women's magazine in the seventies. It has a really simple base of ground coconut with coriander seeds and chilli, which you fry with chickpeas and cooked potatoes. Do look out for the black kala chana specified here in the supermarket – they're small, dark brown chickpeas with a gorgeous texture, and readily available in the World Food or Asian aisles.

MAIN
450g waxy potatoes (e.g. Charlotte),
    peeled and cut into 2.5cm pieces
7–8 fresh curry leaves
1 x 400g tin kala chana chickpeas,
    drained and rinsed
Juice of 1 lemon

STORECUPBOARD
45g desiccated coconut
1 dried red bird's eye chilli
2 teaspoons coriander seeds
2 tablespoons neutral or olive oil
¼ teaspoon mustard seeds
Pinch asafoetida
1 teaspoon sea salt flakes

Cook the potatoes in a large saucepan of boiling water for 8 minutes until just tender. Drain well, then let them steam-dry for a minute.

Meanwhile, tip the coconut, chilli and coriander seeds into a spice grinder or high-speed blender or Nutribullet and blitz for a few seconds until the coconut is quite fine.

Heat the oil in a large frying pan over a medium heat; when hot, add the mustard seeds. As soon as they start to splutter, add the curry leaves and asafoetida and stir-fry for 30 seconds.

Lower the heat, then add the ground coconut mixture and stir-fry for a further 1–2 minutes until the coconut has darkened slightly. Tip in the drained kala chana chickpeas and mix well, then add the cubed potatoes and salt. Very gently toss the potatoes through the chickpeas until they're evenly coated in the coconut spice mix.

Taste for salt, add more if needed, then squeeze over the lemon juice before serving hot. Serve with rice or flatbreads and yogurt for double carbs.

LEFTOVERS: Leftovers are lovely heated through the next day.

EASY FRIED OKRA

Serves: 4   Prep: 10 minutes   Cook: 10 minutes

This is a lovely, simple stir-fried okra recipe with just a few spices – and I can promise it doesn't get sticky! We've found that the best way to keep okra nice and crisp is to wash and dry it thoroughly when still whole before cooking – use a tea towel or kitchen paper so there's no hint of damp before you slice it, and any potential stickiness will be averted. Mum advises that this is her adapted recipe rather than a traditional South Indian one – it's lovely alongside the coconut or lemon rice on pages 66 and 70. Best eaten hot out of the pan.

MAIN
500g okra, washed and thoroughly dried

STORECUPBOARD
3 tablespoons neutral or olive oil
1 teaspoon sea salt flakes
½–1 teaspoon mild chilli powder
1 teaspoon chaat masala
1 teaspoon dried mango powder (amchoor)
1 teaspoon ground coriander seeds
Pinch asafoetida

Cut the thoroughly dried okra into 1cm pieces, discarding the stems.

Heat the oil in a large frying pan and then add the sliced okra. Stir-fry over a medium to high heat for 5 minutes until the edges just start turning brown – don't panic that it looks a little gummy to start with, that'll evaporate off.

Lower the heat (this is important! I burned the spices the first time I made this) and then add the salt, chilli powder, chaat masala, mango powder, ground coriander seeds and asafoetida. Stir-fry for a further minute, then cover with a lid and cook for 5 minutes until the okra is just cooked to al dente. Taste and add more salt as needed.

Serve hot, with rice, naans or flatbread and yogurt.

AVIAL

ONE-POT CARROTS, GREEN BEANS & AUBERGINE
WITH COCONUT & YOGURT

Serves: 6   Prep: 15 minutes   Cook: 25 minutes

I'm not sure you can get a more traditional South Indian dish than avial – a light coconut-based curry finished with yogurt. You can use a variety of different vegetables, including plantain. My favourite is made with chayote (we call it mereka at home), the vegetable that looks like a cute toothless apple. As these aren't very easy to find, Mum often makes this with a mixture of carrots, green beans and aubergine; this is her recipe below. The most important thing is that you cut all the veg the same size – this was my grandfather's job in the kitchen, and I'd be hard pressed to find more perfectly uniform cut vegetables, even in a professional kitchen.

MAIN
2 large carrots, cut into 3cm batons
4 teaspoons tamarind paste
10 fresh curry leaves, roughly torn
200g green beans, topped and tailed
   and cut into 3cm pieces
1 aubergine, cut into 3cm batons
200g Greek yogurt, at room temperature

STORECUPBOARD
½ teaspoon ground turmeric
1 teaspoon sea salt flakes
125g desiccated coconut
1 teaspoon coriander seeds
1 dried red bird's eye chilli
1 tablespoon coconut oil

Take the yogurt out of the fridge – you want it to reach room temperature as you cook.

Put the carrots, tamarind paste, turmeric, curry leaves and salt in a large saucepan. Add just enough water to cover the vegetables, stir, then bring to the boil and cook for 10 minutes.

Add the green beans and aubergine, and a little more water and return to the boil. Cook for a further 10 minutes until the vegetables are all cooked through.

Grind the coconut, coriander seeds and chilli together in a spice grinder or Nutribullet until fine. Add this mixture to the vegetables and simmer for 3–4 minutes to thicken slightly. Turn off the heat.

Beat the yogurt well, then add it to the pan and stir. Heat very gently until you just see a bubble or two break the surface, then turn off the heat – you're treating this with kid gloves as you don't want the yogurt to split. The texture you're after is of vegetables in a light coconut broth, so the consistency of the sauce won't be very much thicker than milk.

Taste for salt and adjust as needed, then stir through the coconut oil before serving hot with fluffy white rice.

AUBERGINE PACHADI

Serves: 4   Prep: 5 minutes, plus 30 minutes standing   Cook: 10 minutes

You can think of this as a sort of South Indian raita – tiny, crisp cubes of aubergine are fried with mustard seeds and curry leaves, scattered with sea salt and served with yogurt as a side dish. If you come across any nice, fresh okra, this is a lovely way to use it as well – just remember to dry the okra thoroughly before slicing it into 1cm pieces and it'll crisp up beautifully in the oil rather than go squashy. Much as I love using the oven instead of the hob, you want the crispness from fried aubergines rather than baked for this dish – and it's quicker to do in a frying pan.

MAIN
1 aubergine, cut into 1cm cubes
6–7 fresh curry leaves
300g natural yogurt

STORECUPBOARD
2 tablespoons neutral or olive oil
1½ teaspoons mustard seeds
½ teaspoon mild chilli powder (optional)
Sea salt flakes

Tip the aubergine cubes into a large bowl with a generous pinch of sea salt, mix well and leave for 30 minutes to draw out the water. (It's not for the bitterness, as modern aubergines aren't particularly bitter, but you get a nicer texture on frying by doing this.)

Drain away any water and pat the aubergine pieces dry with kitchen paper. Heat the oil in a large frying pan, then add the fresh curry leaves and mustard seeds. Turn the heat to medium to low and let the mustard seeds splutter for 30 seconds or so before adding the aubergine cubes. Stir-fry for 6–10 minutes until golden brown and crisp on all sides.

Taste and add sea salt to the aubergines as needed. Spread the yogurt out on a shallow plate or bowl and then scatter over the aubergine pieces. Garnish with chilli powder, if you wish, and serve immediately.

NOTE: You can fry the aubergine cubes in advance and keep them at room temperature for an hour or in the fridge until needed. Heat through in the oven at 160°C fan/180°C/gas 4 for 5 minutes from room temperature or 10 minutes from fridge-cold, before topping the yogurt as above.

SAMBHAR

Serves: 6   Prep: 10 minutes   Cook: 45 minutes

This is one of the most traditional South Indian dals, with just a few spices and tamarind as a seasoning. I like the version with shallots and carrots best, as that's the one my mum makes the most often from my grandmother's recipe – it's perfect served with the dosas on page 212 or just with plain white rice or flatbreads. The tuvar dal lentils are readily available in Asian shops or online, and give the sambhar its characteristic texture. You can use the combination of ground coriander and chilli powder below if you're in a hurry, or make up some of the sambhar powder on page 88 if you have more time.

MAIN

130g tuvar (toor) dal lentils, rinsed well
80g red split lentils, rinsed well
40g tamarind paste
10 shallots, peeled and halved
1 carrot, peeled and sliced into ½cm pieces
10 fresh curry leaves

STORECUPBOARD

1½ teaspoons sea salt flakes
½ teaspoon ground turmeric
1½–2 teaspoons sambhar powder
    (page 88),
    or: 2 teaspoons ground coriander
    1–2 teaspoons mild chilli powder
¼ teaspoon asafoetida
1 tablespoon neutral or olive oil
¼ teaspoon mustard seeds

Put the rinsed lentils in a large saucepan along with 1 litre boiling water, a pinch of salt and the turmeric. Bring to the boil, give it a stir, then cover and simmer over a medium to low heat for 40–45 minutes until the lentils are completely soft. Stir once halfway through the cooking time. Alternatively, this will take 5 minutes on high in a pressure cooker.

While the lentils are cooking, tip the tamarind paste into another large saucepan with the shallots, carrot and 400ml boiling water. Add the sambhar powder (or ground coriander and chilli powder), asafoetida and the remaining 1 teaspoon sea salt flakes. Bring to the boil, then partially cover and simmer for 15 minutes until the carrots are cooked through.

Once the lentils are cooked, whisk them well and then pour the dal into the pan with the tamarind vegetables. Bring the mixture to the boil, then turn off the heat.

To season, heat the oil in a small frying pan over a medium heat; add the mustard seeds and curry leaves when the oil is hot. Let them splutter and pop for 30 seconds, then tip immediately into the dal. Taste and add salt as needed and serve hot.

PALGHAT RASAM

QUICK TOMATO & TAMARIND BROTH

Serves: 4   Prep: 10 minutes   Cook: 20 minutes

Rasam is a delicious tamarind-based broth traditionally added to freshly cooked white rice, with vegetable curries and fried or roasted poppadoms on the side. It can also be served in a small cup as an appetiser before a meal, or as a lovely hot drink on a cold day. There are lots of different versions – I like this one as it's so simple: the everyday rasam that we have at home requires a few tablespoons of cooked dal, which I often don't have ready. This is our version of my aunt Lalitha's recipe.

MAIN
5–6 fresh curry leaves, torn
1 white onion, roughly chopped
1 large vine tomato, roughly chopped
4–5 teaspoons tamarind paste
900ml boiling water

STORECUPBOARD
2 tablespoons neutral or olive oil
½ teaspoon black mustard seeds
1½–2 teaspoons rasam
  or sambhar powder (page 88),
  or: 2 teaspoons freshly ground
  coriander seeds
  ½ teaspoon mild chilli powder
  ½ teaspoon freshly ground black pepper
  Pinch asafoetida
1 teaspoon sea salt flakes

Heat the oil in a medium saucepan; when it's hot, add the mustard seeds. As soon as they start to splutter, lower the heat and add the curry leaves. Let them sizzle for 30 seconds, then add the chopped onion.

Fry the onion over a medium heat for 7–10 minutes until golden brown at the edges, then add the tomato and stir-fry for about 30 seconds.

Add the tamarind paste, boiling water, spices and salt and bring to the boil. Simmer over a low heat for 10 minutes until the tomato is cooked through.

Serve hot with freshly cooked rice and poppadoms on the side, or in cups as a drink.

NOTE: This recipe uses the tamarind paste that you can buy at the supermarket, not the very strong tamarind concentrate from an Asian supermarket (if you have this, just use 2 teaspoons). If you're using a block of tamarind, you'd need a plum-sized portion, soaked in ½ cup of boiling water and then sieved, repeating with a few tablespoons of fresh boiling water until you've got all the extract out.

VEGAN

MOLAGU RASAM

SOUTH INDIAN BLACK PEPPER BROTH

Serves: 2   Prep: 10 minutes   Cook: 10 minutes

This is my favourite rasam; it's so quick to make and exactly what I want when feeling under the weather – the savoury equivalent of a hot toddy. I have fond memories of my parents visiting me in London when I've come down with a bad cold or the flu, and Dad bustling in my tiny kitchen to make this as a remedy. The black pepper gives it a real kick – serve in your favourite glass mug.

MAIN
4 teaspoons tamarind paste
  (see note on page 148)
650ml water

STORECUPBOARD
½ teaspoon black peppercorns
¼ teaspoon ground turmeric
1 teaspoon sea salt flakes
¼ teaspoon ground cumin

Tip the black peppercorns into a pestle and mortar and grind them fairly coarsely.

Put the tamarind paste, ground peppercorns and 300ml of the water in a medium-sized saucepan along with the turmeric and salt and bring to the boil. Lower the heat and simmer for 5 minutes.

Add the remaining water gradually – you're doing this to taste, so for a stronger flavour add less water – and bring back to the boil. Turn off the heat and stir through the ground cumin. Taste and adjust the salt, and serve hot.

LEFTOVERS: If you don't drink this all in one go, pop the leftovers in the fridge and warm through the next day.

COCONUT, TAMARIND & CURRY LEAF BROTH

THAENGA ARACHU KOZHAMBU

Serves: 6   Prep: 15 minutes   Cook: 25 minutes

This is one of my favourite South Indian dishes; think of it as a dal, but without the lentils. The flavours from just a few ingredients – tamarind, curry leaves and spiced coconut – come together beautifully in this light accompaniment to rice. If you spot curry leaves in the supermarket, this is the perfect dish to make with them. Leftovers can be frozen.

MAIN

4 heaped teaspoons tamarind paste
15 fresh curry leaves, roughly torn
800ml boiling water
7 small shallots, peeled and halved
2 teaspoons black split urad dal
200g Greek yogurt, at room temperature
50ml cold water

STORECUPBOARD

1 teaspoon sea salt flakes,
 or to taste
1½ teaspoons oil
2 teaspoons coriander seeds
1 dried red bird's eye chilli
100g desiccated coconut
¼ teaspoon black mustard seeds

Put the tamarind paste, 10 of the curry leaves, boiling water, shallots and salt in a large saucepan and bring to the boil. Simmer for 10 minutes until the shallots are cooked through. (Small round shallots will cook in this time: banana shallots will take a further 5–6 minutes.)

Meanwhile, heat ½ teaspoon of the oil in a small frying pan, then add the urad dal, coriander seeds and chilli. Toast over a medium to low heat for 2–3 minutes until the chilli has darkened and the spices smell lovely and aromatic.

Tip the toasted spices into a spice grinder or Nutribullet with the desiccated coconut and grind until fairly fine. Add the coconut spice mix to the pan with the tamarind and shallots, bring to the boil, then simmer for a further 5 minutes before turning off the heat.

Beat the yogurt well with the cold water, then add it to the pan and stir. Heat very gently until you just see a bubble or two break the surface, then turn off the heat – you don't want the yogurt to split. Taste for salt and adjust as needed.

Heat the remaining teaspoon of oil in the small frying pan; when hot, add the mustard seeds and remaining curry leaves. Cook over a medium heat until the mustard seeds 'pop', then immediately tip the contents of the pan into the broth. Serve with plenty of fluffy white rice.

NOTE: The best way to peel shallots, if you have the small round type rather than long banana shallots, is to put them in boiling water for 5 minutes. Once halved, the skins will slip off easily.

SOME TRADITIONAL BENGALI DISHES

ALOO DUM
BENGALI POTATO CURRY
WITH SPICED TOMATOES (V)

DIDU'S DIMER JHAL
MUSTARD EGGS WITH SPRING ONIONS
& TURMERIC (V)

CHECHKI
ONE-TIN SPICED CAULIFLOWER
& POTATO CURRY WITH PEAS (VG)

MASOOR DAL (VG)

GHONTO
BENGALI CABBAGE & POTATO CURRY (V)

CHINGRI MACHER MALAI CURRY
PRAWN MALAI CURRY (P)

DOI MAACH
FISH WITH YOGURT & TURMERIC (P)

DIDIMA'S BEGUN KALONJI
BABY AUBERGINES WITH YOGURT
& NIGELLA SEEDS (V)

SOME TRADITIONAL BENGALI DISHES

'Tomatoes and potatoes: Bengalis put them in everything!'
Parvati Iyer (my mum)

There's only one thing that Bengalis enjoy more than eating, and that's talking about food. They are also evangelical about fish – which type is the best in season, how to prepare it, and what to serve with it. On our visits to Kolkata, I've had, among other dishes, fish seasoned with mustard, wrapped in banana leaves and steamed, fish cooked in a yogurt sauce, and prawn cutlets, where you butterfly prawns and bash them out, then marinate them in Worcestershire sauce, vinegar and spices before crumbing and frying. My mum's favourite birthday meal was always prawn cutlets, served with homemade crisps, fried rice, ketchup and kasundi – Bengali mustard sauce. Size-wise, the prawns in West Bengal are somewhere between a langoustine and a small lobster – when a Bengali aunt looked at the cooking times in a newly gifted *Roasting Tin*, the first thing she queried was how a prawn could cook in 5 minutes, so I had to explain the size difference. She commiserated.

I've included a simpler version of prawn cutlets in the snack chapter on page 30 (accounting for the difference in size) and my version of Bengali mustard fish appears on page 102. Doi maach, a lovely simple dish of fish cooked in yogurt, is in this chapter on page 174 – I like to use salmon, but you'd traditionally use a firm-fleshed white fish.

It's traditional in West Bengal for the man of the house to go out to the market and choose the fish himself, before handing it over to be cooked at home (and there'll be long conversations on the best way to cook it). Within the meal itself, fish is just one component – a traditional Bengali meal runs the full gamut of flavours, starting with something bitter and finishing with something sour before a sweet. My mum's estimated breakdown (and this is just for one meal) is: 1) a saag (leafy greens) with kasundi, 2) a vegetable dish served with rice, 3) a dal and something crunchy, 4) a fish dish (meat and fish on a Sunday) and 5) sweet yogurt to finish. And that's just for lunch! Dinner might consist of different types of bread, such as puris, luchis and parathas, served with vegetable curries.

My Bengali late grandmother, who we called Didu, was an exceptionally good cook. When my mum was growing up, she would make both Bengali and Western dishes on special occasions, using recipes clipped out from magazines or a well-loved American cookbook for the latter. She no doubt inherited her abilities from my great-grandmother Didima, who was also a brilliant cook – it's her recipe for the begun kalonji, aubergines with yogurt & nigella seeds, on page 176. Mum recalls how Didu improvised an oven so she could make roast chicken and bread and butter puddings for the children – oven cooking still isn't particularly prevalent in India, so it's all the more impressive that she was doing this back in the sixties. I had the opportunity to learn a few recipes from her myself a few years back, and include her recipe for nimbu pani – sweet lime juice with just a pinch of salt – on page 224. Her recipe for prawn cutlets has turned into the Bengali popcorn shrimp on page 30.

ALOO DUM

BENGALI POTATO CURRY WITH SPICED TOMATOES

Serves: 4–6 as a side   Prep: 15 minutes   Cook: 35 minutes

This is my mother's recipe for the classic Bengali potato curry. It's so simple to put together – you can use Jersey Royals when in season, otherwise use the smallest whole potatoes that you can find. Unusually for my standard 'minimal fuss' approach, I recommend the mindful task of peeling the potatoes after they're boiled, which is how I was brought up to do them (eventually, and slightly mutinously, asking why we didn't just use a potato peeler). But I've come to agree that shape-wise, the potatoes do look best when prepared this way, but you can definitely peel them before cooking if you're in a hurry. Serve with puris or luchis (page 192), green peas kachori (page 198), rice or flatbreads.

MAIN
600g Jersey Royals
  or other small new potatoes
1 teaspoon butter or ghee
2 onions, finely chopped
2 cloves garlic, grated
10 cherry tomatoes, quartered
200ml hot water
Fresh coriander, to serve

STORECUPBOARD
1 tablespoon oil
1 cinnamon scroll
4 green cardamom pods, bashed
4 cloves
2 bay leaves
½ teaspoon ground turmeric
1½ teaspoons mild chilli powder
1 teaspoon sea salt flakes, or to taste
1 teaspoon sugar

Bring a large saucepan of water to the boil and add the unpeeled potatoes. Cook for 10–15 minutes until they're just cooked through and tender to a fork (they'll take more or less time depending on the size of the potatoes). Drain well, cool in a bowl of cold water and then peel. (You can enlist a partner or small child to help with this bit.)

Meanwhile, heat the oil and butter or ghee in a large frying pan over a medium heat and add the cinnamon scroll, cardamom pods, cloves and bay leaves. Fry for a minute until the bay leaves darken, then add the onions and garlic. Cook over a medium to low heat for 10 minutes, stirring frequently, until the onions soften and just start turning golden brown around the edges.

Add the turmeric, chilli and salt, stir-fry for a further 30 seconds, then add the cooked potatoes and stir gently to coat them in the spiced onions. Add the tomatoes, water and sugar and stir again, then simmer for 10 minutes until the flavours have blended. Taste and add salt as needed, and serve hot.

DIDU'S DIMER JHAL

MUSTARD EGGS WITH SPRING ONIONS & TURMERIC

Serves: 4   Prep: 10 minutes   Cook: 25 minutes

If you like mustard, you'll love this easy Bengali egg curry. My mum and I road-tested it with freshly ground mustard seeds versus grainy Dijon mustard: while she agreed that the freshly ground mustard seed version was more authentic, we thought the version with Dijon was easier (and it's my preferred option). If you want to make this the authentic way, grind a teaspoon of mustard seeds in a pestle and mortar until bright yellow, mix with a teaspoon of water and use it in place of the Dijon.

MAIN

4 medium free-range eggs,
  at room temperature
1 onion, finely chopped
1 inch ginger, grated
2 heaped teaspoons grainy Dijon mustard
120ml boiling water
6 spring onions, trimmed
  and cut into 3cm pieces

STORECUPBOARD

2 tablespoons neutral or olive oil
1 teaspoon panch phoron (page 87),
  or use equal parts/what you have
  of nigella, fennel, mustard, fenugreek and
  black cumin seeds to make up 1 teaspoon
½ teaspoon ground turmeric
1 teaspoon sea salt flakes, or to taste

Pop the eggs into a saucepan of boiling water and cook for 10 minutes. Drain, then leave to cool in a bowl of cold water. Peel and halve when cool enough to handle.

Meanwhile, heat the oil in a large frying pan over a medium heat and add the panch phoron. Lower the heat and fry for 30 seconds, then add the chopped onion. Cook over a medium to low heat for 10 minutes, stirring occasionally, until golden brown.

Add the turmeric and ginger to the onions, stir-fry for a further minute, then add the Dijon mustard along with the boiling water. Bring to the boil, then add the salt, spring onions and halved, boiled eggs, cut side facing upwards. Spoon some of the sauce over the cut side of the eggs, then cover and cook for 5–6 minutes over a medium to low heat until the spring onions are cooked through. The sauce should be thin, just coating the egg and onions.

Taste the sauce for salt, then serve with white rice, chapattis or flatbreads.

CHECHKI

ONE-TIN SPICED CAULIFLOWER & POTATO CURRY WITH PEAS

Serves: 4   Prep: 15 minutes   Cook: 40 minutes

Chechki is a classic Bengali dish, where cauliflower and potatoes are cooked with panch phoron or Bengali five-spice. Traditionally, you'd make this in a frying pan, cooking the potatoes and cauliflower with the spices from raw. While this is delicious, it's very time-consuming, so over the years Mum and I have adapted this to an easy one-tin version, which saves so much time and lends a lovely flavour and colour to the potatoes and cauliflower. It's wonderful served with the puris or luchis on page 192 or shop-bought parathas, which you can buy and cook from frozen.

MAIN

1 medium cauliflower,
   cut into small florets
400g potatoes, peeled
   and cut into 1cm cubes
175g frozen peas, defrosted
Fresh coriander leaves, to serve

STORECUPBOARD

3 tablespoons neutral or olive oil
1 teaspoon sea salt flakes, or to taste
2½ teaspoons panch phoron (page 87),
   or use equal parts/what you have
   of nigella, fennel, mustard, fenugreek
   and black cumin seeds to make up
   2½ teaspoons
1 teaspoon sugar

Tip the cauliflower and potatoes into the roasting tin, mix well with the oil, salt and panch phoron, then transfer to the oven and cook for 30 minutes until the potatoes and cauliflower are cooked through and lightly brown.

Add the defrosted peas and sugar, stir, then return to the oven for a further 10 minutes. Taste for salt, adjust as needed, then scatter with fresh coriander before serving hot.

NOTE: It's not traditional in Bengal to use the cauliflower leaves in this dish, but you can if you wish. (Just don't tell my mum.)

MASOOR DAL

Serves:4–6   Prep: 10 minutes   Cook: 30 minutes

This is one of the very simplest dals that you can make, and you'd find it on the table every day in a Kolkata household. It's very soothing; traditionally you'd serve it with lime wedges and a green chilli on the side (my aunts on both sides have been known to crunch the green chilli up just as it is). This dal is lovely with freshly cooked white rice with butter or ghee, but you could also serve it with chapattis or flatbreads.

MAIN
150g red lentils, rinsed well
600ml boiling water
1 fresh red or green chilli, slit lengthways
1 onion, thinly sliced
Fresh coriander and lemon or lime wedges,
    to serve

STORECUPBOARD
½ teaspoon ground turmeric
2 tablespoons neutral or olive oil
1 teaspoon cumin seeds
1 bay leaf
Sea salt flakes, to taste

Tip the lentils, boiling water and turmeric into a large saucepan and bring to the boil. Once it's boiling, cover with a lid, turn the heat down to low and cook for 30 minutes until the lentils are soft, stirring occasionally so they don't stick to the bottom of the pan.

When you have 10 minutes left on the lentils, heat the oil in a medium frying pan and add the cumin seeds and bay leaf. Stir-fry for 30 seconds until aromatic, then add the chilli and onion. Cook over a medium heat for 10 minutes, stirring frequently, until the onions are a deep golden brown and starting to crisp at the edges.

Once the lentils have had 30 minutes, whisk them well with a good pinch of salt so they're nice and smooth. Tip the hot, cooked onions in with the lentils, stir once and taste. Adjust the salt as needed, then scatter over the fresh coriander and serve with the lemon or lime wedges on the side to squeeze over before you eat.

NOTE: If you're going to eat all the dal immediately, you can season with lemon or lime juice to taste in the pan. But if you're going to keep some for the next day (it keeps really well in the fridge for a couple of days and can be frozen), season with lemon just before serving, as it can turn bitter when stored.

GHONTO

BENGALI CABBAGE & POTATO CURRY

Serves: 6 generously Prep: 15 minutes Cook: 30 minutes

This is such a lovely mixed vegetable curry, where lightly cooked cabbage takes centre stage in a perfectly balanced mix of spices along with potatoes, peas and tomatoes. Delicious with a bowl of fluffy white rice, or bought parathas cooked from frozen.

MAIN
1 small sweetheart cabbage,
 finely shredded
2 medium potatoes (400g), peeled
 and cut into 2.5cm cubes
2 vine tomatoes, sliced
120g frozen peas, defrosted
1 teaspoon ghee or butter

FOR THE GARAM MASALA
3 black cardamom pods
4 cloves
¼ cinnamon scroll

STORECUPBOARD
3 tablespoons neutral or olive oil
1 teaspoon cumin seeds
2 bay leaves
½ teaspoon ground turmeric
1 teaspoon mild chilli powder
2 teaspoons ground ginger
1 teaspoon ground cumin
2 teaspoons ground coriander
1 teaspoon sugar
1 teaspoon sea salt flakes

Start by making the garam masala – you just need to tip the black cardamom pods, cloves and cinnamon scroll into a spice grinder or Nutribullet and blitz until fine. You'll need 2 teaspoons for this recipe – keep the rest in a small jar for another recipe.

Put the cabbage in a wok or large non-stick saucepan with 400ml boiling water. Cover and let it steam on a medium heat for 3–4 minutes, then drain the cabbage in a colander.

Wipe out the wok or saucepan and add the oil. Tip in the raw potatoes and fry until golden brown all over – this will take about 3 minutes per side over a medium to high heat, about 15 minutes in total. Remove them from the pan, and set aside. Add the cumin seeds and bay leaves to the pan, and fry over a medium heat for 30 seconds to 1 minute until the cumin seeds start to brown, then lower the heat and add the rest of the spices, the sugar and salt. Stir for a minute, add the sliced tomatoes, and cook for 3–4 minutes.

Add the steamed cabbage, fried potatoes and peas. Stir to cover the potatoes with the cabbage and cook, uncovered, over a medium heat for a further 5–7 minutes until the potatoes are cooked through. Add salt to taste and adjust as needed, then add 2 teaspoons of the garam masala along with the ghee or butter, stir and cover until ready to serve.

CHINGRI MACHER MALAI CURRY

PRAWN MALAI CURRY

Serves: 4   Prep: 10 minutes   Cook: 25 minutes

This was one of my mum's favourite prawn curries before she became vegetarian – a lovely, lightly spiced dish of prawns cooked in coconut milk; my grandmother would always have it made for her on visits home. This is my version of a classic Bengali recipe by Pragya Sundari Devi, known as Kolkata's Mrs Beeton. In her cookbook, published in the early 20th century, she wrote definitive versions of Bengali classics as well as Victorian recipes of the time, like mock-turtle soup. I love this as it takes just minutes to put together – perfect served on a weeknight with buttery white rice alongside.

MAIN
2 tablespoons butter, ghee or oil
2 large onions, finely chopped
2 cloves garlic, grated
2 inches ginger, grated
1 red chilli, finely chopped
1 x 400ml tin coconut milk
360g raw king prawns
Juice of 1 lime
Fresh coriander, to serve

STORECUPBOARD
½ cinnamon scroll
5 cloves
3 green cardamom pods, bashed
½ teaspoon ground turmeric
1 teaspoon sea salt flakes

Heat the butter, ghee or oil in a large frying pan, then add the cinnamon scroll, cloves and cardamom pods. Fry over a medium heat for 30 seconds or so until fragrant, then add the chopped onions. Cook the onions for 10 minutes, stirring occasionally, until golden brown around the edges.

Add the grated garlic, ginger, chilli, turmeric and salt and stir-fry over a low heat for a further 2–3 minutes before adding the coconut milk. Bring to the boil, then lower the heat and simmer for 8 minutes until thickened.

Add the prawns and cook for a further 3–4 minutes until the prawns are pink and cooked through. Squeeze in the lime juice, taste and adjust the seasoning and serve hot scattered with the fresh coriander.

DOI MAACH

FISH WITH YOGURT & TURMERIC

Serves: 6   Prep: 10 minutes, plus 2 hours marinating   Cook: 35 minutes

This is such a simple, classic Bengali dish, and takes just minutes to put together after you marinate the fish. I've adapted it to cook in the oven, as I find the yogurt keeps its silky texture best that way, and used salmon in place of the traditional freshwater rohu. You could definitely use any other type of firm, white-fleshed fish – monkfish is lovely for a special occasion. Serve with freshly cooked white rice with a little butter stirred through.

MAIN
250g natural yogurt
6 salmon or thick white fish fillets
2 white onions, roughly chopped
2 inches ginger, grated
2 cloves garlic, grated
1 green chilli, finely chopped
Fresh coriander leaves, to serve

STORECUPBOARD
½ teaspoon ground turmeric
1 teaspoon mild chilli powder
2 tablespoons neutral or olive oil
1 bay leaf
4 cloves
3 green cardamom pods, bashed
¼ cinnamon scroll
Sea salt flakes, to taste

Mix the yogurt with the turmeric, chilli powder and a pinch of salt. Place the fish in a roasting tin large enough to hold everything in one layer, then spoon half the yogurt mixture over the fillets. Cover and marinate in the fridge for 1–2 hours.

When you're ready to cook, preheat the oven to 180°C fan/200°C/gas 6. Heat the oil in a large frying pan over a medium heat and add the bay leaf, cloves, cardamom pods and cinnamon scroll. Lower the heat and stir-fry for a minute until the bay leaf has lightly browned.

Add the chopped onions, ginger, garlic and green chilli with a pinch of sea salt, then stir-fry over a medium heat for 10 minutes until golden brown around the edges. Turn off the heat, and let the onions cool for 5 minutes before stirring in the remaining yogurt.

Spoon the onion and yogurt mixture on and around the marinated fish, then transfer to the oven to bake for 20–25 minutes until the fish is just cooked through.

Taste the sauce and add salt as needed, then scatter with the fresh coriander leaves before serving hot.

NOTE: To cook this the traditional way on the hob, place the marinated fish into the frying pan with the cooked onions and yogurt mixture. Cover and cook over a low heat for 15–20 minutes until the fish is just cooked through.

DIDIMA'S BEGUN KALONJI

BABY AUBERGINES WITH YOGURT & NIGELLA SEEDS

Serves: 2 as a main, 4 as a side   Prep: 10 minutes   Cook: 20 minutes

I love this recipe for a number of reasons: firstly, it's delicious and really easy to make – the aubergines sit in a beautiful combination of spices in a yogurt sauce which comes together in just 20 minutes, most of that hands-off time. Secondly, the recipe comes from my great-grandmother, Didima; my grandmother transcribed and sent it on wafer-thin blue airmail paper to my mum in the UK, who translated the recipe for me as we cooked it together. It's traditionally served on special occasions and best eaten immediately – lovely with the puris on page 192 or flatbreads.

MAIN
6 long, thin baby aubergines
125g Greek yogurt, at room temperature

STORECUPBOARD
1 teaspoon ground turmeric
1½ teaspoons ground coriander seeds
½ teaspoon mild chilli powder
1 teaspoon sea salt flakes
2 tablespoons neutral or olive oil
1 teaspoon nigella seeds

Cut the baby aubergines in half lengthways to about 2.5cm below the stem, so they're still attached at the top.

Mix 1 heaped teaspoon of Greek yogurt with the turmeric, ground coriander seeds, chilli powder and a pinch of salt. Use the teaspoon to rub a little of this thick spice paste inside each of the split aubergines.

Mix the remaining spice paste with the rest of the Greek yogurt and salt and set aside.

Heat the oil in a large frying pan; when hot, add the nigella seeds. Stir-fry for 30 seconds until aromatic, then add the aubergines. Give them a quick turn in the hot oil, then turn the heat right down, cover and cook for 7 minutes. Turn the aubergines over, then cover and cook for a further 7 minutes until they're cooked through (if you prod them with a fork, they should be soft through).

Turn off the heat and spoon the yogurt sauce all over the aubergines. Return the pan to the heat and reheat over a very low heat for 3–4 minutes just to cook through the spices – you want it on the very lowest heat possible so the yogurt doesn't split.

Taste the sauce to check for salt, adding a tiny pinch if needed, and serve hot.

PANEER

HOW TO MAKE PANEER

Makes: 1 ball   Prep: 5 minutes, plus 1–2 hours draining   Cook: 15 minutes

This is such an easy two-ingredient recipe, and perfect to make the paneer kofta on page 208. If you're just making the paneer to have at home, you could mix it through with sea salt and chopped soft herbs like coriander, chives or parsley, or let it set and then cut it into 2cm cubes to fry or roast as in the recipe on page 108. I also like to use it as a stuffing – just crumble it and mix with chilli, ground cumin, salt and lemon juice, stuff the mixture into halved mini peppers and roast, drizzled with a little oil.

MAIN

2.25 litres whole milk
   (you must use whole milk!)
Juice of 2 lemons

Pour the milk into your largest saucepan or stockpot – you want a good few inches of pan left above the level of the milk, as the milk loves to try to boil over. Bring to the boil over a medium heat, stirring the bottom of the pan occasionally – this will take 10–15 minutes from cold.

Once the milk has come to the boil, let it bubble up furiously for 15–30 seconds before adding the lemon juice. Let it boil for a further 15 seconds, then turn off the heat and stir. The milk should immediately 'split', leaving you with creamy milk solids and the thin, watery whey. Carefully pour the mixture into a sieve lined with a clean muslin or j-cloth, set over the sink, then bring the ends of the j-cloth up to enclose the solids. Twist into a tight ball, secure with string or a rubber band, and hang on a cupboard door set over a bowl for 1–2 hours to let the excess liquid drain away.

After a couple of hours the paneer should be nice and firm. It is now ready to use for kofta or as a stuffing for mini peppers: use immediately, or store in the fridge for up to 2 days. If you want to cut it into cubes to fry or roast, leave it in the fridge to firm up overnight.

WEEKEND
PROJECTS

PURIS
(OR LUCHIS) (VG)

BEGUN BHAJA
CRISPY FRIED AUBERGINE (VG)

CHOP
CHEESE-STUFFED POTATO CAKES (V)

GREEN PEAS KACHORI (VG)

BONDAS
CRISP POTATO, CURRY LEAF & MUSTARD SEED BITES (VG)

MURUKKU (VG)

METHU VADA (VG)

MALAI KOFTA (V)

SAFFRON, ALMOND & PANEER FESTIVAL PULAO (V)

DOSA (VG)

WEEKEND PROJECTS

For someone who publicly advocates hassle-free cooking, I have an enduring and contradictory love for crisp, deep-fried food. Think of this chapter as a love-letter to deep-frying, as well as to a slow weekend kitchen potter – after all, if you enjoy cooking and have the time to do it, it's lovely to follow a new recipe without the usual pressure of getting dinner on the table as you would post-work on a weeknight.

The recipes in this chapter are a real treat – from the North Indian puris (or Bengali luchis) on page 192, which you absolutely must serve with the begun bhaja on page 193 – forgive me for a second, I actually don't have words to describe how good the soft, puffed-up bread is with the crisp, fried aubergine rounds, and am getting really hungry writing this – to the green peas kachori on page 198, where a simple spiced pea filling sits inside a very similar puri dough. Both make incredible special occasion lunches.

South Indian recipes, like my grandmother's recipes for murukku (crisp, savoury rice twists) on page 202 and methu vada (fluffy lentil doughnuts) on page 204 are the most incredible snack food, and again something to make when you have a bit of time on your hands, and fancy experimenting with a new, hands-on recipe. I've included the recipe for my grandmother's dosas (fermented rice and lentil pancakes, page 212) in this chapter, as although they aren't deep-fried and are quite simple to make, they are a weekend project by virtue of the long fermentation period.

For the deep-fried recipes, there are a number of safety tips that you absolutely must keep in mind – see overleaf. Part of the reason I'm so comfortable deep-frying is that I've watched my mum do it so many times, so if you'd like, you can watch my video cooking the pakoras from page 26 by following the link at the end of the book, on page 266. I promise that once you get the hang of it, it isn't too much of a hassle, and done at the correct temperature (180°C) the food shouldn't take in too much oil. I do get a lot of satisfaction pouring the cold oil back into the bottle after cooking, and seeing that it's only a couple of tablespoons down on the original amount.

TOP TIPS FOR SAFE DEEP-FRYING

DO

> Use a large saucepan or wok, and never fill it more than half full.

> Keep the pan on one of the back burners of the hob,
> not at the front (to avoid knocking the handle).

> Keep the handle of your pan angled away from you
> (and ideally don't touch it).

DON'T

> Don't let the oil get too hot – three-quarters of the maximum
> heat of your induction/gas/electric hob is fine.

> Don't overcrowd the pan – anything you put in will make the oil
> bubble up, so err on the side of less, and cook in batches.

> Don't leave the pan unattended at any point.

> Don't let children anywhere near the hob.

> Don't ever move a pan of hot oil. When you're finished,
> let the oil cool down completely.

AND

> If the oil starts to smoke, it's too hot. Turn off the heat immediately.

> It's not a bad idea to keep a fire blanket and extinguisher
> in your kitchen just in case.

ADDITIONALLY

> Use fresh oil – oil that's been used too many times will taint the food and isn't good for you. I'd use a pan of oil for a maximum of two lots of deep-frying before disposing of it safely (see next tip) and just once if anything floury has gone in.

> Used cooking oil shouldn't go down the sink; it'll ruin your drain. When cold, use a funnel or carefully pour the oil back into the bottle it came in, and close it tightly. You can recycle used cooking oil at your local recycling centre.

> Use a nice big slotted metal spoon to lift your cooked food out, and keep a plate lined with kitchen paper nearby to drain it. But not too near a gas flame, as you don't want the paper to catch fire.

OR

> You could just get a deep fat fryer. But still bear all the above safety tips in mind!

PURIS
(OR LUCHIS)

Makes: 12   Prep: 15 minutes, plus 30 minutes resting for the dough   Cook: 10 minutes

Arguably one of the best types of Indian bread – these light, puffed-up pillows will disappear in seconds. Our family motto is 'don't count how many you're eating, just eat' – though my dad and his brothers would on occasion have competitions as to who could eat the most in one sitting. I recommend these as a 'make with a friend' activity – one of you can roll while the other fries – Mum and I had 12 of these done in minutes working as a team (it took her considerably longer when we were kids and less useful at rolling/deep-frying). Based on Madhur Jaffrey's recipe, these puris are perfect with the crispy fried aubergine on page 193.

MAIN	STORECUPBOARD
110g wholemeal chapatti flour	30ml vegetable oil
110g plain flour	
100ml water	1 litre vegetable oil, for deep-frying

Tip the flours, water and 30ml vegetable oil into a food processor and blitz – it'll look like couscous initially, but keep the machine running a little longer and it'll turn into a smooth dough. Try not to add any extra water, as you don't want it to get sticky.

If you don't have a food processor, rub the oil into the flours with your fingertips until rubbly, then slowly mix through the water and knead for about 5 minutes until you have a soft dough. Place the dough in an oiled bowl, then cover with clingfilm and let it rest for 30 minutes.

When you're ready to cook, divide the dough into 12 pieces and roll each into a ball. Keep them covered in clingfilm. Heat the oil in a large saucepan, filling it no more than half full. When the oil has reached about 180°C – when a cube of bread dropped in sizzles and turns golden brown within 30 seconds – you're ready to roll.

On an oiled surface, roll a piece of dough into a neat circle, about 10cm in diameter. Carefully lower the circle into the hot oil and, with a slotted metal spoon, gently press down on the centre of the circle. This will help it to puff up. Cook for about 15–30 seconds on each side – it will look obviously 'cooked' and turn a lovely pale golden brown – then carefully lift it out with the slotted spoon. Tap the spoon against the side of the pan to get rid of the excess oil, then drain on a plate lined with kitchen paper.

Continue with the remaining dough – this is easiest if you have a friend roll while you fry (or vice versa). Eat them while hot, as quickly as you can.

NOTE: You can make these with all plain white flour, in which case they are called luchis.

BEGUN BHAJA

CRISPY FRIED AUBERGINE

Serves: 2–3   Prep: 5 minutes, plus 10 minutes standing   Cook: 12 minutes

My family is divided over this dish: my sister, Mum and I love it, and my dad inexplicably does not. (But on the plus side, there's more crisp, fried aubergine for us to eat.) All you have to do is slice rounds of aubergine, season them with salt and turmeric before lightly dusting in flour and deep-frying – addictively good. They're the perfect accompaniment for the puris on page 192. If you're having them together, which is a very Bengali thing to do, I'd recommend frying the puris in the hot oil first, and then these immediately afterwards. This can easily be scaled up if you're feeding more people – just double the recipe below.

MAIN
1 aubergine, cut into 1.5cm thick slices

STORECUPBOARD
1 teaspoon sea salt flakes
1 teaspoon ground turmeric
2 tablespoons plain flour

1 litre vegetable oil, for deep-frying

Rub each side of the cut aubergine pieces with the sea salt and turmeric, then set aside for 10 minutes.

When you're ready to fry, heat the oil in a large saucepan, filling it no more than half full. When the oil has reached about 180°C – when a cube of bread dropped in sizzles and turns golden brown within 30 seconds – lightly dust each aubergine slice in the flour and then gently lower 2–3 pieces of aubergine into the oil and lower the heat to medium.

Fry the aubergine for 2 minutes on each side until golden brown and crisp. Use a slotted metal spoon to transfer them to a plate lined with kitchen paper and continue until you've fried all the aubergine pieces.

Serve hot, ideally with the puris or luchis on page 192. These would also make an excellent snack, dusted with a pinch more sea salt flakes.

CHOP

CHEESE-STUFFED POTATO CAKES

Makes: 12   Prep: 30 minutes   Cook: 30 minutes

Chop are a Bengali snack brought about during the British rule in Kolkata, where local chefs would come up with Indianised versions of traditional British dishes. What started out as a rissole in the UK became a fried potato cake stuffed with spiced minced lamb, banana blossom or jackfruit in Kolkata. Watching my mum make the banana blossom version as a child, I asked if we could stuff the chop with cheddar cheese instead. The answer was a resounding yes – they've been on my birthday menu for the last 30 years. Fantastic with the coriander chutney on page 36.

MAIN

800g floury potatoes (I use Maris Piper),
 peeled and cut into 2.5cm cubes
100g cheddar, cut into 12 cubes
40g plain flour with a pinch sea salt
75g panko breadcrumbs, lightly crushed
1 medium free-range egg, beaten

STORECUPBOARD

1 teaspoon sea salt flakes
½–1 teaspoon mild chilli powder

1 litre sunflower or neutral oil, for deep-frying

Bring a large saucepan of water to the boil and cook the potatoes for 10 minutes until cooked through. Drain well, then return to the pan to steam-dry for 5 minutes. Mash the potatoes until smooth, then stir through the salt and chilli powder. Taste and adjust as needed. When cool enough to handle, take a heaped tablespoon of the mash and flatten in your palm. Place a cube of cheese in the middle, then pat the mash around it to form a small, flat cake. Transfer to a tray lined with baking paper and repeat to make 12 cakes.

Tip the flour and panko breadcrumbs into 2 separate, shallow bowls alongside a bowl with the beaten egg. Dip and turn each potato cake evenly into the flour, then the egg, then the breadcrumbs – this is easiest if you use one hand for the egg and the other for the flour and panko. Place each chop back on the lined tray as you continue. At this stage, you can cook the chop or refrigerate them for a few hours/overnight until needed.

When you're ready to cook, pour the oil in a large saucepan to no more than half full and heat to 180°C, or until a cube of bread sizzles and turns a pale golden brown within 30 seconds. Lower the heat to medium, then gently lower in 3–5 chop (or however many will comfortably fit in one layer leaving plenty of space) and fry for 2–3 minutes on each side until golden brown and crisp. Use a slotted metal spoon to transfer them to a plate lined with kitchen paper as you go, and continue until they're all fried. These can be kept warm in a low oven until you're ready to serve, or reheated in the oven if you're making them a little in advance.

GREEN PEAS KACHORI

Makes: 16   Prep: 25 minutes, plus 30 minutes resting for the dough   Cook: 15 minutes

Bengali kachori are slightly different from the crisp, savoury biscuit-style kachori in other regions of India – this version is soft and fluffy, similar to the puris on page 192 with a simple but delicious pea filling. This recipe comes from Renu, a spectacular cook who helps my aunt in her home in Kolkata – they're addictively good, and wonderful served with aloo dum and cauliflower chechki (pages 162 and 166). Double-carbing is traditional with this dish.

FOR THE DOUGH
220g plain flour
100g wholemeal chapatti flour (atta)
2 tablespoons oil (or ghee if not vegan)
¼ teaspoon bicarbonate of soda
¼ teaspoon finely ground black pepper
1 teaspoon sea salt flakes
Small squeeze of lemon juice
185ml water

FOR THE FILLING
200g frozen peas
1 tablespoon neutral or olive oil
1 teaspoon finely grated ginger
1 teaspoon sea salt flakes
1 teaspoon ground roasted cumin seeds
  (page 86)

1 litre sunflower or neutral oil, for deep-frying

Tip the plain flour, chapatti flour, oil, bicarb, black pepper, sea salt and lemon juice into a large bowl. Slowly add the water bit by bit, and stir to bring into a stiff dough (you may need a fraction more or less water depending on how absorbent/new/old your flour is, so go slowly). Knead the dough for 5 minutes, then cover and leave to rest for 30 minutes.

While the dough is resting, cook the peas in a saucepan of boiling salted water for 5 minutes. Drain well, then mash as smoothly as you can with a potato masher. Set aside.

To finish the filling, heat the oil in a small frying pan and add the grated ginger. Stir-fry for 30 seconds, then add the peas and stir-fry for 2–3 minutes until the water has evaporated. Add salt to taste, stir through the ground roasted cumin seeds and leave to cool.

Divide the dough into 16 pieces. Flatten each piece in your hand to a small cup and stuff with a teaspoon of the pea filling. Bring the edges of the dough around the filling and twist to enclose completely. Gently roll into a ball and repeat with the remaining dough, covering them with clingfilm as you go.

When you're ready to cook, pour the oil into a large saucepan until no more than half full and heat to about 180°C, or until a cube of bread dropped in sizzles and turns golden within 30 seconds. Lightly oil a work surface and roll each piece of dough out to about 8cm in diameter. Gently lower into the hot oil and prod with a slotted spoon to encourage it to puff up. Cook for about 30–45 seconds, and then flip it over to cook for a further 30 seconds, before removing to a plate lined with kitchen paper. These are best eaten very soon after cooking. (The filled, uncooked dough, however, will keep well covered in the fridge for an afternoon.)

BONDAS

CRISP POTATO, CURRY LEAF & MUSTARD SEED BITES

Serves: 6   Prep: 20 minutes   Cook: 25 minutes

Bondas are a brilliant South Indian snack, a bit like pakoras, but with a spiced mashed potato filling. They're incredibly moreish and perfect to serve before a bigger meal, or with drinks. If you fry them ahead of time, they can be warmed through in the oven before serving, but they're best eaten straight out of the pan.

FOR THE FILLING
800g potatoes, peeled
   and cut into 2cm cubes
1 tablespoon neutral or olive oil
½ teaspoon black mustard seeds
6–7 fresh curry leaves
½ teaspoon mild chilli powder
½ teaspoon ground turmeric
Pinch asafoetida
Sea salt flakes, to taste

FOR THE BATTER
112g gram (chickpea) flour
45g rice flour
½ teaspoon mild chilli powder
½ teaspoon sea salt flakes
150ml water

1 litre vegetable oil, for deep-frying

Bring a large saucepan of water to the boil and cook the potatoes for 10 minutes until they're cooked through. Drain well, then let them steam-dry for 5 minutes.

Meanwhile, heat the tablespoon of oil in a small frying pan; when hot, add the mustard seeds and curry leaves. Lower the heat and let them splutter for 30 seconds before adding the chilli powder, turmeric and asafoetida. Stir for a further 30 seconds, then mix the spices and oil through the potatoes and crush roughly with salt to taste. When cool enough to handle, form into small golf-sized balls. At this stage, you can refrigerate the mash until needed.

For the batter, mix the flours, chilli powder and sea salt flakes together in a bowl. Gradually add the water until you have a batter about the consistency of single cream.

When you're ready to fry, heat the oil in a large saucepan over a medium heat, filling it no more than half full. Once the oil has reached 180°C, or when a cube of bread dropped in sizzles and starts to turn golden within 30 seconds, you're ready to fry. Working in batches, dip 5–6 potato rounds into the bowl with the batter, then lower gently into the hot oil. Fry over a medium heat for 4–5 minutes until golden brown and crisp – you'll know it's done as the oil will stop bubbling so fiercely. Use a large slotted metal spoon to transfer the bondas to a plate lined with kitchen paper, then continue with the remaining potato rounds and batter. Serve hot.

VEGAN

MURUKKU

Serves: 6–8   Prep: 10 minutes   Cook: 25 minutes

These are one of my dad's favourite snacks, and my grandmother would make them for him (as part of a wider selection) every birthday. It's a really simple dough of rice and gram flour, fried until crisp. The only slightly technical aspect is the gadget used to press the dough out into shapes in the hot oil – I bought a specific murukku or sev press, which are readily available online, but if you have a cookie press or cylindrical icing set with a star-shaped nozzle, that would work well too.

MAIN
160g rice flour
140g gram (chickpea) flour
150ml cold water

STORECUPBOARD
½ teaspoon sea salt flakes
¼ teaspoon mild chilli powder
¼ teaspoon bicarbonate of soda

1 litre vegetable oil, for deep-frying

Tip the rice flour, gram flour, salt, chilli powder and bicarb into a large bowl. Slowly add the cold water and stir together to form a stiff dough.

When you're ready to fry, pour the oil into a large saucepan no more than half full. Heat until it reaches 180°C, or until a cube of bread dropped in sizzles and turns golden within 30 seconds.

Break off sections of the dough and put them in your murukku/cookie press fitted with a star-shaped attachment. Very carefully press out two to three circles of dough straight into the hot oil – just do one or two to start with to get the feel of it; you don't want to overcrowd the pan.

Fry the murukku for 2–3 minutes until golden brown and crisp. Use a large slotted spoon to transfer them to a plate lined with kitchen paper and continue until you've used up the dough.

These are lovely hot or cold. Anything you don't eat immediately can be cooled to room temperature and stored in an airtight tin for a week.

METHU VADA

Makes: 10   Prep: 15 minutes, plus 4 hours soaking   Cook: 30–40 minutes

If you've never tried these fluffy little savoury doughnuts, you're in for a treat. This is my grandmother's recipe; all you need is a bowl of soaked white lentils, a few spices and a food processor. Fry one or two at a time to judge the heat of the oil and texture of the vadas (which should be lovely and spongy, a bit like bread), and then when you're confident you can fry four at a time like a pro. Excellent snack food – they go really well with the coriander chutney on page 36 or natural yogurt.

MAIN
220g white urad dal, rinsed well
5 fresh curry leaves
2 inches ginger, finely grated
2 green chillies, finely chopped

STORECUPBOARD
1 teaspoon sea salt flakes

1 litre sunflower or neutral oil, for deep-frying

Tip the rinsed lentils into a large bowl and cover with roughly twice their volume of warm water. Cover and leave to soak for 4 hours. Once the lentils have had 4 hours, drain them well, then transfer to a food processor and blitz until you have a smooth, thick, dough-like paste. Stir in the curry leaves, ginger, chillies and salt. You can now store the paste in the fridge until you're ready to fry.

When you're ready to cook, get a large tray and line it with clingfilm. Have a bowl of water handy and wet your hands before breaking off a large walnut-sized portion of the paste. Roll it into a ball (easy with wet hands, impossible with dry) and poke a hole through the middle with your finger to make a doughnut shape, then transfer to the lined tray. Repeat with the remaining dough: you should have 10 in total.

Pour the oil into a large saucepan, filling it no more than half full, and heat over a medium heat to 170°C. Gently lower in 2–3 vadas and cook for 5 minutes each side until golden brown and crisp on the outside, using a large slotted metal spoon to encourage them off the bottom of the pan if they stick. You're looking for a long, slowish fry here rather than a quick in-and-out, because if the outside browns too quickly, the inside won't fluff up and cook, so take your time and err on the side of lowering the heat – test the first one out of the pan as a cook's perk, and adjust your temperature for the rest accordingly.

Once they're golden brown and have had 10 minutes in the pan, use a metal slotted spoon to fish the vadas out, carefully shaking off the excess oil, and transfer to a plate lined with kitchen paper. Continue with the remaining dough, and serve hot.

MALAI KOFTA

Serves: 6   Prep: 25 minutes, plus time to make the paneer   Cook: 40–50 minutes

This is a special celebration dish, with beautifully spiced, fluffy paneer kofta in a cream-enriched tomato sauce. I request it every birthday (it goes very well with the cashew nut pulao on page 76) and while it requires a little bit of kitchen pottering to make the paneer, the quick tomato sauce can be made and frozen ahead, the paneer made and refrigerated ahead of time, with the two warmed separately and put together just before serving.

FOR THE SAUCE
2 tablespoons oil
1 onion, roughly chopped
1 inch ginger, grated
2 heaped teaspoons freshly ground
  coriander seeds
1 teaspoon ground cumin
1 teaspoon mild chilli powder
1 teaspoon sea salt flakes
2 tablespoons desiccated coconut
1 x 400g tin chopped tomatoes
100ml single cream

FOR THE KOFTA
1 x batch homemade paneer
  (page 181)
10g fresh coriander leaves,
  plus extra to serve
1 red or green chilli, stem removed
2 tablespoons plain flour
½ teaspoon bicarbonate of soda
1 heaped teaspoon sea salt flakes

1 litre vegetable oil, for deep-frying

Heat the 2 tablespoons of oil in a large saucepan and add the onion. Stir-fry over a medium heat for 10 minutes until golden brown at the edges. Lower the heat and add the ginger, spices, salt and coconut and stir-fry for a further 2–3 minutes.

Tip the onion mixture into a food processor or high-speed blender and blitz to a paste. If it's too thick to blend, add half the chopped tinned tomatoes. When smooth, add the remaining tomatoes and blitz until completely smooth. Return the onion and tomato mixture to the pan and bring to the boil. Add the cream, then lower the heat and simmer for 10–15 minutes. Taste and adjust the salt as needed.

For the kofta, tip the paneer into a food processor with the coriander leaves, chilli, flour, bicarb and sea salt flakes. Blitz briefly until the mixture looks like couscous, then with lightly oiled hands, form into 20–25 small kofta, each about two-thirds the size of a golf ball.

Heat the oil in a large saucepan, filling it no more than half full. Let it heat to about 170°C, or until a cube of bread dropped in sizzles and just starts to turn golden within 30 seconds. Fry the paneer kofta in batches for about 2 minutes on each side until a light golden brown, using a large slotted metal spoon to turn them halfway. Transfer to a plate lined with kitchen paper and continue frying the rest of the kofta, turning down the heat if they brown too quickly. Set aside or cool and refrigerate until needed. Just before serving, reheat them in the oven for 6 minutes at 160°C fan/180°C/gas 4.

Reheat the sauce, add in the kofta, garnish with fresh coriander, and serve immediately.

SAFFRON, ALMOND & PANEER FESTIVAL PULAO

Serves: 4   Prep: 20 minutes   Cook: 30 minutes

This is such a lovely festive rice dish – the saffron and cardamom give it a wonderful, luxe flavour, and the butter-fried almonds and paneer kofta work beautifully with it. While making the homemade paneer kofta takes a little time, the rice itself is an easy 20-minute one-pan dish which you could easily make without the kofta for a simpler weekend meal. This looks really lovely brought to the table in a wide, flat bowl.

MAIN
1 x batch paneer kofta (page 208)
50g salted butter
100g blanched almonds
200g basmati rice
350ml water
Fresh coriander, to serve

STORECUPBOARD
5 cardamom pods, bashed
Large pinch good saffron threads,
    steeped in 1 tablespoon boiling water
1 heaped teaspoon sea salt flakes

You will need: a saucepan
    with a tight-fitting lid

You can make and fry the paneer kofta following the paneer recipe on page 181 and kofta recipe on page 208 up to a day ahead. Take them out of the fridge when you start this recipe.

For the rice, heat the butter in a saucepan with a tight-fitting lid. Add the almonds and cardamom pods and fry for 3–4 minutes over a medium heat until the almonds are golden brown.

Meanwhile, steep the saffron threads in the boiling water.

Add the basmati rice to the butter and almonds and stir-fry the rice for a further 2 minutes. Add the 350ml water, saffron mixture and salt and bring to the boil. Cover with a lid, lower the heat right down and cook for 15 minutes without removing the lid. Once cooked, take the lid off and use a fork to fluff through the rice. Let it steam-dry uncovered for 5 minutes, then taste for salt.

To serve, warm the kofta through for 5 minutes at 160°C fan/180°C/gas 4 from room temperature, or for 10 minutes from fridge-cold. Transfer the rice to a warm dish, stir through the kofta and scatter over the fresh coriander before serving hot.

NOTE: Do use the best saffron you can find: I find the Belazu brand consistently good and wonderfully aromatic, but other supermarket brands of saffron less so.

VEGAN

DOSA

Serves: 4   Prep: 15 minutes   Soaking and fermenting: 48 hours   Cook: 25 minutes

This is my grandmother's recipe for the traditional South Indian fermented rice and lentil pancakes. Like breadmaking, it takes a little time for the batter to ferment, but it's easily done as a weekend project – soak the rice and lentils overnight on Friday (5-minute job), blitz the mixture in a food processor on Saturday morning (10-minute job), and let the batter rise and get bubbly somewhere warm until Sunday dinnertime. Thicker than the paper dosas you get in restaurants, they're delicious with the sambhar on page 146, gunpowder spice on page 91, or my favourite, with a little sugar.

MAIN
400g long-grain rice, rinsed
200g white urad dal, rinsed

STORECUPBOARD
½ teaspoon fenugreek seeds

Vegetable or neutral oil, for frying

Put the rice and the lentils in 2 large separate bowls, with half the fenugreek seeds in each. Cover both with several times their volume of cold water, then cover and leave to soak overnight.

The next morning, drain the water from the lentils and pop them in a food processor or high-speed blender with 250ml water. Blitz until completely smooth, then transfer to a large mixing bowl.

Drain the water from the rice, then pop half of it into the food processor with 100ml water and blend until completely smooth. Scrape it out into the blended lentil mix, then repeat with the remaining rice and another 100ml water. Stir all three mixtures together in the mixing bowl along with another 50ml water until you have a thick batter. Cover with clingfilm and leave to ferment somewhere warm for 36 hours until bubbly and well risen.

You can keep the fermented batter in the fridge, covered, for up to 3 days until you're ready to cook, or use it straight away.

To cook the dosas, heat a teaspoon of oil in a large, heavy-based frying pan over a low heat, then pour half a ladleful of batter into the centre. Using the rounded base of the ladle, smooth the batter out using a circular motion from the middle of the pan outwards, to form a large, thin circle. Increase the heat to medium to high, dot the top of the batter with a further teaspoon of oil and cook for a minute before flipping over as soon as the top looks 'set'. Cook for a further minute, then remove and continue with the remaining batter. Best eaten straight out of the pan.

SWEETS & DRINKS

LEMON, GINGER & TURMERIC SUNSHINE TONIC (V)

SALTED LASSI (V)

MANGO & CARDAMOM LASSI (V)

NIMBU PANI (VG)

CHAKRAI PONGAL
SOUTH INDIAN RICE PUDDING WITH JAGGERY & CASHEW NUTS (V)

REALLY SUPERB PEANUT BRITTLE (V)

SHAHI TUKRA
BREAD & BUTTER PUDDING (V)

MANGO, STEM GINGER & LIME ICE CREAM (V)

CARDAMOM, YOGURT & PISTACHIO ICE CREAM (V)

ROASTED CUMIN & LEMON SHORTBREAD (V)

SWEETS & DRINKS

Sweets are the second (or possibly joint-first) favourite food in Bengal, and the Indian code of hospitality requires that guests eat until they have to be rolled out of the house, or they risk causing mortal offence. This is problematic for visitors without a sweet tooth (me), diabetics (my dad) and people who are recently out of pre-diabetes (my mum). But on our most recent visit to Kolkata, we arrived during the Bengali harvest festival of Poush Sankranti, when really special sweets are made out of the first-press date palm jaggery gur – equivalent to the best maple syrup, but only available once a year. There was one absolutely spectacular sweet on offer called gokul pithe, which was so good that I ordered seconds at a restaurant – they're little steamed rice-flour dumplings, stuffed with a mixture of the special jaggery and freshly grated coconut, and served in a sweet condensed milk sauce. I later learned that they'd been lightly deep-fried, not steamed, which is why they were so nice compared to the other versions. Other classic Bengali sweets include sondesh, sweets made from cottage cheese and sugar which will send most Bengalis into raptures just at the mention of them, and special nolen gurer sondesh made with the first-press jaggery gur. You can now get seasonal nolen gur ice cream too, which Mum highly recommends. I write about these sweets here without including recipes, because as with classic French pastries, it's unusual for people to make them at home unless they have a special interest or lots of spare time – Bengalis would go to a good sweet shop instead, of which there are plenty in Kolkata.

But some Indian sweets are easy to make at home – I include here sweet chakrai pongal, a classic Tamilian rice pudding (page 226), again made with jaggery (but you can use brown sugar too), and the extremely popular peanut brittle (page 228). Cumin in shortbread (page 236) might sound a little unusual, but sweet jeera biscuits are extremely popular in India – I like to make a batch of these to go with either of the ice creams at the end of the chapter. Because I'm often running late when people come over for dinner, I've started handing over the unbaked shortbread dough to any visiting child along with a box of cookie cutters, asking if they'd like to help make pudding. It goes down well as an alternative to colouring in, and it's a robust enough dough to stand up to rolling and rerolling into dinosaurs, penguins, stars etc.

LEMON, GINGER & TURMERIC SUNSHINE TONIC

Serves: 2   Prep: 5 minutes, plus 10 minutes steeping

If anyone at home has even the vaguest sniff or cough, I make them this tonic; inspired by the ideas in Mira Manek's book *Prajna*, it's packed with turmeric, ginger, black pepper and lemon. My mother swears it's helped her feel better when under the weather (or perhaps she's just trying to avoid my making her a second cup), but as a home remedy for a sore throat, I feel the colour of the drink alone will make you feel better – I have it whenever I need some extra oomph in the morning. I like to drink this hot as tea, with or without honey.

MAIN
2 inches unpeeled ginger (about 25g)
2 inches unpeeled fresh turmeric (about 8g)
1 lemon, sliced

STORECUPBOARD
½ teaspoon black peppercorns
½ cinnamon scroll, broken
5 cloves
Honey or agave syrup, to taste

Blitz the ginger, turmeric and peppercorns in a high-speed blender or Nutribullet, using a little water if you need it to help them blend. Alternatively, you can pound them by hand in a pestle and mortar. Tip the mixture into a teapot, along with the cinnamon scroll, cloves and lemon slices. Cover with boiling water, and leave to steep for 10 minutes. Strain into cups or sturdy glasses, adding honey or agave syrup to taste.

NOTE: You will need to bear in mind that fresh turmeric stains, so don't wear your (or your dad's) best cashmere jumper, and wipe up any spills immediately.

SALTED LASSI

Serves: 2   Prep: 5 minutes

I always order salted lassi at Indian restaurants – a much better partner for food than sweet – and it helps to have alongside particularly spicy food, as I have pretty much zero chilli tolerance. It's perfect for hot weather too – well worth making double and stashing it in the fridge for a refreshing drink throughout the day.

MAIN
½ teaspoon ground roasted cumin
  (or ½ teaspoon cumin seeds; see below)
300g fridge-cold natural yogurt
100ml cold water

STORECUPBOARD
Big pinch sea salt flakes, crushed

If you're roasting and grinding cumin seeds from scratch, tip ½ teaspoon cumin seeds into a small frying pan and toast over a medium heat for a couple of minutes until aromatic. Let them cool down a little, then grind in a pestle and mortar into a fine powder.

Whisk the yogurt, water and salt together in a jug with most of the ground roasted cumin and taste for salt. Add a pinch more if needed, then pour into 2 glasses.

Scatter over the remaining ground roasted cumin and serve immediately.

NOTE: You can serve this on ice if you wish.

MANGO & CARDAMOM LASSI

Serves: 4–6 Prep: 10 minutes

There are two ways to make mango lassi – with good fresh mangoes or with bought tinned Alphonso mango pulp. I find the latter much more reliable in flavour – head to the World Food aisle at your local big supermarket, the section with largeish bags of rice and lentils and you'll inevitably find large tins of extremely good tinned Alphonso or Kesar mango pulp (also available in their online aisles). But I give both methods below, so you can use fresh or tinned mangoes as you prefer – perfect served over ice on a hot day.

FRESH MANGO LASSI

4 good ripe mangoes,
    peeled and roughly chopped
4 cardamom pods, seeds lightly ground
500g natural yogurt or kefir
Honey or agave syrup, to taste

TINNED MANGO LASSI

1 x 850g tin Alphonso/Kesar mango pulp
4 cardamom pods, seeds lightly ground
500g natural yogurt or kefir

For the fresh mango lassi, tip the roughly chopped mango, ground cardamom seeds (I use a pestle and mortar to quickly grind them) and yogurt or kefir into a high-speed blender or Nutribullet. Blitz until smooth and then taste – if your mangoes aren't very sweet, you may wish to add a little honey or agave syrup – and blitz again. Taste and adjust the sweetness as needed, then serve over ice.

For the tinned mango lassi, pour the mango pulp into a large jug and add the ground cardamom seeds and yogurt or kefir. Stir well with a wooden spoon and serve over ice. (There's enough sweetness in the tinned mango that you won't need extra honey.)

LEFTOVERS: I inevitably make the quantity above, which would do six, just for the two of us – store the leftovers in a jug in the fridge for up to 2 days.

NIMBU PANI

Serves: 2   Prep: 15 minutes   Chill: 2 hours

This is my grandmother Didu's recipe – think of the best freshly squeezed lemonade you've ever had, but made with limes and a tiny pinch of salt. It's so refreshing and moreish, particularly on a hot day. I give quantities to serve two below so you don't get banned from the supermarket for buying up all the limes, but you can easily scale it up if you're serving more people.

MAIN
5 unwaxed limes
120g white caster sugar
200ml water
Pinch sea salt flakes
Ice, mint sprigs and lime slices, to serve

Zest the limes into a medium saucepan, add the sugar and 80ml of the water, then place over a low heat for 5 minutes, stirring occasionally, until the sugar has dissolved. Set aside to cool.

Use the palm of your hand to squash and roll the whole limes against a work surface a few times – it'll help release the juice. Halve and juice them into a bowl or large jug – you need 120ml for this recipe, so juice another lime if needed, or save the spare lime juice for another dish if you have a bit more.

Mix 120ml of the cooled sugar syrup with the 120ml lime juice and add in the remaining 120ml cold water and a pinch of sea salt. Stir well, then taste – it should taste strong, sweet and sour all at the same time, so add in fractions more sugar syrup, water and lime juice to taste. But bear in mind you're going to chill it in the fridge, so the stronger it tastes now the better, as the cold will slightly mute the flavours.

Strain through a sieve into a clean jug, and chill for 2 hours, or until needed. Serve over ice, with mint sprigs and lime slices to garnish if you wish.

CHAKRAI PONGAL

SOUTH INDIAN RICE PUDDING WITH JAGGERY & CASHEW NUTS

Serves: 2–4   Prep: 10 minutes   Cook: 30 minutes

This is one of my dad's favourite puddings, which is traditionally made for the South Indian harvest festival of Pongal when the new-season jaggery (palm sugar) is harvested. When he showed me how to make it, I thoroughly approved of his liberal chef-like use of butter at pretty much every stage (along with the very chef-like trait of tidying away as he went along). We checked the recipe on the phone with my grandmother's sister, my great-aunt Leela Chithi in Trivandrum – she recommends 250g sugar in this recipe, but we decided to halve it – feel free to increase it as you wish!

MAIN

1 tablespoon split moong dal

100g American long-grain
   or basmati rice, rinsed

400ml water

125g jaggery or soft dark brown sugar

3 teaspoons butter

30g cashew nuts, halved

40g raisins

STORECUPBOARD

8 cardamom pods, seeds only

Tip the moong dal into a small frying pan, and toast over a low heat for about 4 minutes until aromatic. Meanwhile, grind your cardamom seeds in a pestle and mortar.

Put the rice, half the ground cardamom, 300ml of the water and the toasted moong dal into a saucepan with a tight-fitting lid and bring to the boil. Cover, then lower the heat and cook for 18 minutes until the rice is cooked through and slightly sticky (you're not going for al dente with this one).

Meanwhile, tip the jaggery or sugar, remaining ground cardamom and 100ml water into a large saucepan and bring to the boil. Simmer for 3–4 minutes until the jaggery or sugar has melted and the syrup has slightly thickened. Tip the cooked rice and dal mixture into the syrup and simmer for 5 minutes, stirring frequently. Add a teaspoon of butter.

In the frying pan you used to toast the dal, heat the remaining 2 teaspoons of butter. Add the cashew nuts and fry for 3–4 minutes over a medium to low heat until golden brown, then add the raisins and fry for a further minute until they've plumped up. Stir the buttery cashew nuts and raisins through the rice, reserving a few to scatter over if you wish. Serve warm.

REALLY SUPERB PEANUT BRITTLE

Makes: plenty!   Prep: 5 minutes   Cook: 25 minutes, plus 1 hour setting

Peanut brittle, or peanut chikki, was one of my mum's favourite snacks growing up – you can buy massive slabs of it in corner shops in India. It's made with jaggery rather than sugar, but you could use either for this recipe. As always with caramel making, it's easiest if you have a sugar thermometer, but if not, dropping teaspoons of the hot caramel into cold water to see what happens is a good indication too (see below). I like to non-canonically use a mixture of salted and unsalted peanuts for a grown-up edge – do use the freshest you can find.

MAIN
150g unsalted peanuts
100g salted peanuts
250g jaggery or soft dark brown sugar
130ml water
1 teaspoon butter

STORECUPBOARD
5 green cardamom pods, seeds only

Preheat the oven to 160°C fan/180°C/gas 4.

Tip both lots of peanuts into a shallow baking tray and roast for 10 minutes until aromatic. Set aside to cool. Line another small, shallow baking tray with greaseproof paper (one the size of a Swiss roll tin is perfect).

Meanwhile, grind the cardamom seeds in a pestle and mortar and pop them into a saucepan along with the jaggery or sugar and water. Place over a medium heat until the sugar has dissolved, then increase the heat and bring the syrup to the boil. Don't stir it – you can use a heatproof pastry brush dipped in cold water to gently brush down the sides of the pan to get rid of any sugar which might burn.

Bring the syrup up to the 'hard crack' stage – when you drop the hot caramel into a glass of cold water, it forms hard, brittle threads. (This is a stage on from forming a 'hard ball' that doesn't squash too much when you squeeze it, and two stages on from a 'soft ball' which easily squashes out of shape.) This takes me just under 15 minutes at a rolling boil.

Tip the butter into the hot caramel, and then the roasted peanuts. Stir quickly, then pour the mixture out on to your lined baking tray. Let it cool for 30 minutes before scoring into squares, and for a further 30 minutes before cutting through completely.

SHAHI TUKRA

BREAD & BUTTER PUDDING

Serves: 6–8   Prep: 15 minutes   Cook: 25–30 minutes

Shahi tukra is a rich Mughal dessert, where crisp butter-fried bread is soaked in a cardamom-and-saffron-infused milk. In the interests of speed (and greed) I decided to convert it into a brioche bread and butter pudding, so you get a crisp topping along with the wonderful flavours of saffron and cardamom within the dish – blackberries and pistachios are my left-field addition. My mother serves the original with clotted cream on the side, and so as not to break with tradition, I give it as a serving suggestion here.

MAIN
50ml milk (whole or semi-skimmed)
3 medium free-range egg yolks
85g caster sugar
300ml single cream
400g sliced brioche, cut into quarters
150g blackberries
Handful chopped pistachios
Clotted cream, to serve

STORECUPBOARD
Generous ½ teaspoon good saffron threads
6 cardamom pods, seeds ground

Preheat the oven to 150°C fan/170°C/gas 3.

Heat the milk in a small saucepan and add the saffron. Turn off the heat and let it infuse.

Meanwhile, whisk the egg yolks with the caster sugar, single cream and ground cardamom seeds. Arrange the sliced brioche and blackberries in a buttered roasting tin or flan dish and pour over the eggy custard.

Use the back of a teaspoon to mash the saffron into the milk (this will release more colour), and then carefully drizzle this all over the pudding. Scatter with the pistachios and then transfer to the oven to bake for 25–30 minutes until golden brown and crisp on top. Serve immediately with clotted cream.

NOTE: Do use the best saffron you can find: I find the Belazu brand consistently good and wonderfully aromatic, but other supermarket brands of saffron less so.

MANGO, STEM GINGER & LIME ICE CREAM

Serves: 8   Prep: 20 minutes   Chill and freeze: 5 hours to overnight

This is such a gorgeous ice cream, studded with crystallised ginger and with a hint of lime bringing out the very best of the mango. As with the recipe for mango lassi on page 222, when ripe Indian or Pakistani mangoes aren't in season, I urge you to make this ice cream with the readily available Alphonso or Kesar mango pulp in a tin (as they come in 850g tins, you can use up the remaining pulp for a lassi). Perfect to serve after dinner.

300g tinned mango pulp from a tin
300ml double cream
Zest and juice of 2 limes
5 medium free-range egg yolks
90g caster sugar
120g crystallised ginger, chopped

Gently heat the mango pulp and cream in a saucepan with the lime zest, stirring until it just comes to the boil, then turn off the heat.

Whisk the egg yolks and sugar in a bowl until smooth, and then pour over the hot mango cream, stirring continuously.

Return the mango custard to the pan and stir over a medium to low heat for 5–6 minutes until thickened – it should coat the back of a spoon (this means when you run your finger through the back of a spoon then tip it from side to side, the liquid is thick enough that it won't run).

Let the mixture cool for 20 minutes, then stir through the lime juice. Let the custard cool to room temperature, then chill in the fridge for at least an hour before churning, following the instructions on your ice-cream machine. Add the chopped crystallised ginger about 5 minutes before the ice cream is ready.

If you don't have an ice-cream machine, you can pour the mixture into a shallow container and pop it in the freezer. Fork it through every hour to break up the ice crystals (repeat this every hour for 4–5 hours), adding the crystallised ginger and stirring through on the final mix. Return to the freezer; when you're ready to eat, let it sit at room temperature for 20 minutes before serving.

CARDAMOM, YOGURT & PISTACHIO ICE CREAM

Serves: 8   Prep: 20 minutes   Chill: 5 hours to overnight

This ice cream is a variation on a lockdown recipe that I made for my dad, who requested cardamom ice cream when I wanted to make some sugar-free versions for him. The addition of the ground pistachios gives this a wonderful, kulfi-like flavour, and I love that it's just a few easily available ingredients. It's now a staple when we have friends or family round.

MAIN
400ml double cream
5 medium free-range egg yolks
150g natural yogurt
100g pistachios

STORECUPBOARD
7 cardamom pods, seeds ground
100g caster sugar

Pour the cream into a saucepan, add the ground cardamom seeds and place over a low heat until it just comes to the boil, then turn off the heat.

Whisk the egg yolks and sugar in a bowl, then pour over the hot cream, stirring continuously.

Return the cream and egg mixture to the pan and stir over a medium to low heat for 4–5 minutes until thickened – it should coat the back of a spoon (this means when you run your finger through the back of the spoon then tip it from side to side, the liquid is thick enough that it won't run). Strain the mixture into a clean bowl, then stir through the yogurt. Let the custard cool to room temperature.

While the custard is cooling, preheat the oven to 160°C fan/180°C/gas 4. Toast the pistachios in the oven for 10 minutes, and let them cool completely. Tip the nuts into a high-speed blender or Nutribullet and blitz until quite fine (don't overblitz though, as the nuts will get oily – think ground almond texture). Stir the pistachios through the cardamom custard and refrigerate for 1 hour.

When the ice-cream base is chilled, churn it in your ice-cream machine following the manufacturer's instructions. Either serve straight away or chill in the freezer before serving.

If you don't have an ice-cream machine, you can pour the chilled mixture into a shallow container and pop it in the freezer. Fork it through every hour to break up the ice crystals, and repeat this every hour for 4–5 hours. Refreeze, and when you're ready to eat, let it sit at room temperature for 20 minutes before serving.

NOTE: For a sugar-free version of this, substitute the sugar with 50g xylitol.

ROASTED CUMIN & LEMON SHORTBREAD

Serves: 6–8   Prep: 20 minutes, plus 1 hour chilling   Cook: 15 minutes

Cumin may sound like an unusual addition to a biscuit dough, but sweet cumin or jeera biscuits are so popular in India – perfect with a cup of tea from a roadside tea-stall. As I mention in the spice chapter (page 86), dry-roasting cumin seeds has a transformative effect on their scent and flavour, which makes all the difference here. They work beautifully served with either of the ice creams in this chapter, or any of the masala chai variations on page 20.

MAIN
100g softened butter
50g caster sugar
Zest of 1 lemon
110g plain flour
40g rice flour

STORECUPBOARD
1 teaspoon cumin seeds

Tip the cumin seeds into a small frying pan and toast over a low heat for 2–3 minutes, shaking the pan frequently, until aromatic. Allow to cool for a minute or so, then roughly grind in a pestle and mortar.

In a large bowl or stand mixer, beat the butter, sugar and lemon zest together until pale and fluffy. Gently fold in the flours and the ground cumin, bringing the mixture together into a soft dough as quickly as you can. Form the dough into a neat round, then wrap and chill in the fridge for 1 hour.

When you're ready to bake, preheat the oven to 160°C fan/180°C/gas 4 and line a baking tray with baking paper.

On a lightly floured surface, gently roll out the dough with a floured rolling pin to about 3mm thick and stamp out shapes of your choice. (The dough isn't terribly precious about the way it's handled – I've given the dough to children to roll and stamp out with excellent results.)

Transfer the shapes to the lined baking tray, reroll and stamp out the remaining dough, then transfer to the oven to bake for 15 minutes, keeping an eye after 12 minutes if you have smaller shapes. When cooked, the biscuits should take on hardly any colour, but look firm and feel sandy to the touch. Gently transfer to a wire rack to cool and serve with ice cream or tea. These will keep well in an airtight container for 3–4 days.

NOTE: As with all shortbread, rice flour lends these biscuits a fantastic crisp texture, but you can use all plain flour if that's what you have in the cupboard.

MENUS

MENUS

WEEKEND BRUNCH

Spiced caramel chai (page 20)

Mini's masala frittata (page 48)

Beetroot, curry leaf & ginger buns (page 50)

Quick-cook utthapam with tomatoes, onions & coriander (page 58)

Mango & cardamom lassi (page 222)

DRINKS PARTY

Pankaj's addictive chilli peanuts with lime (page 22)

Sticky spiced popcorn (page 24)

Crunchy street-food chaat with tamarind & coriander chutney (page 36)

Tandoori roasted sweetcorn (page 106)

A BENGALI-STYLE DINNER PARTY

WITH DRINKS: Cheddar, cumin & nigella seed straws (page 28)

Chop (page 194) served with coriander chutney (page 36)

Begun kalonji – aubergines with yogurt & nigella seeds (page 176)

Roasted cauliflower with mustard, chilli & lemon (page 110)

Aloo dum (page 162)

Cashew nut pulao rice (page 76)

Shahi tukra bread & butter pudding (page 230)

MENUS

A SOUTH INDIAN-STYLE DINNER PARTY

WITH DRINKS: Murukku (page 202)

Bondas (page 200)

Aubergine pachadi (page 144)

Keralan potato curry with chickpeas & coconut (page 138)

South Indian-style black pepper & fennel prawns (page 128)

South Indian puy lentil & broccoli stir fry (page 122)

Tamilian lemon rice (page 70)

Cardamom, yogurt & pistachio ice cream (page 234)

DINNER FOR FAMILY, FRIENDS & CHILDREN

Nimbu pani (page 224)

Bengali popcorn shrimp (page 30)

Mini-naan pizzas with lime & coriander paneer (page 52)

Green pea, cauliflower & onion pulao (page 72)

Aubergine, tomato & nigella seed curry (page 96)

Chickpeas with tamarind, kale & ginger (page 124)

Mango, stem ginger & lime ice cream (page 232)

STORE
CUPBOARD

STORECUPBOARD

I imagine you'll have most of the ingredients you need for the recipes in this book in your cupboard already: these are the basics that'll see you through most of the book, along with some of the more unusual ingredients for project cooking.

OIL

I have mostly written 'neutral oil' in the ingredients list throughout the book rather than specifying the type, because while my mum always uses rapeseed oil for Indian food, and would have used sunflower or vegetable oil in the past, I use light olive oil for almost everything in the kitchen. It's fine to use whatever you have (other than extra virgin olive oil, which would be too strongly flavoured and obviously not the flavour profile you want for Indian food). I buy in organic sunflower oil or similar for deep-frying.

SALT

Always Maldon in my house, as I know exactly how salty the flakes will be. Mum doesn't think this is quite right for Indian food and uses fine sea salt instead, but all the recipes in the book were tested with Maldon, bearing in mind that it is less salty than fine sea salt, so 1 teaspoon sea salt flakes will be about as salty as ½ teaspoon fine sea salt.

RICE

Basmati for pretty much every recipe in the book, and occasionally American long-grain for the South Indian recipes. See the intro to the rice chapter on page 63 re rice brands.

STORECUPBOARD

FLOUR

A small bag of wholewheat chapatti flour (atta) is useful if you're going to make the puris (page 192), but you can use ordinary plain white flour and then they're known as luchis. Plain white flour is fine for the parathas (page 56).

You'll need gram flour and rice flour for the pakoras (page 26) and a few of the deep-fried dishes in the book.

LENTILS

This book is fairly light on lentils – a bag of Egyptian red lentils will see you through the mainstream recipes.

A couple of the more involved recipes include tuvar (toor) dal, chana dal, moong dal and white split urad dal – I'd get these on an ad hoc basis from an Asian grocery shop or a supermarket's World Food aisle.

CHICKPEAS/RED KIDNEY BEANS

Tins are fine for either of these; if you're being fancy or it's a special occasion, you can get the Navarrico ones in a jar.

Kala chana, or small brown chickpeas, are worth looking out in the World Food aisle of your local supermarket; they're really lovely with tamarind and a nicer texture than regular tinned chickpeas.

TAMARIND

It's fine to buy the little jars that you get at the supermarket, they're convenient if a little pricey. If you're making anything involving tamarind frequently, you're better off getting a semi-soft 'brick' from the World Food aisle or an Asian grocey shop, soaking golf-ball-sized amounts in a little boiling water, and then pressing the pulp through a sieve with the back of a spoon.

STORECUPBOARD

BROWN ONIONS, RED ONIONS, GINGER, GARLIC

Essential for Indian food (though garlic isn't used by my dad's family), I'm never without any of these. Fresh turmeric is optional: I tend to use ground in curries and save fresh just for drinks (page 218).

FRESH CURRY LEAVES, FRESH MINT, FRESH CORIANDER

Fresh curry leaves can be hit and miss to get hold of – an Asian grocery shop will have them in person or online, and some large branches of major supermarkets do stock them as well (I've had success in Waitrose, Sainsbury's, Asda and Tesco before).

Fresh mint and coriander – easy to get. I can never keep fresh coriander alive in those little growing pots so tend to buy the biggest bag I can from the supermarket, wrap it in damp kitchen roll and store in a bag or box in the fridge. This keeps mint fresh for ages too.

LEMONS & LIMES

Saving the best till last, I'm never without either. A spritz will lift the flavours in most dishes, and when you think something needs salt, it often needs citrus. Buy unwaxed if you're using the zest.